W9-BAN-238

Jewish Holidays and Festivals

Jewish Holidays and Festivals

Jewish Holidays and Festivals

by DR. ISIDOR MARGOLIS

and RABBI SIDNEY L. MARKOWITZ

ILLUSTRATIONS BY JOHN TEPPICH

THE CITADEL PRESS

NEW YORK

630477 c 2

BURLINGTON COUNTY LIBRARY
MOUNT HOLLY, NEW JERSEY

FIRST PRINTING

COPYRIGHT © 1962 BY ISIDOR MARGOLIS AND SIDNEY L. MARKOWITZ
ALL RIGHTS RESERVED
LIBRARY OF CONGRESS CATALOG CARD NUMBER 62-19769
MANUFACTURED IN THE UNITED STATES OF AMERICA
PUBLISHED BY THE CITADEL PRESS
222 PARK AVENUE SOUTH, NEW YORK 3, N. Y.

THIS BOOK

IS DEDICATED TO OUR WIVES

EDNA MARGOLIS   AND   RUTH G. MARKOWITZ

WHOSE ENCOURAGEMENT AND SELF-DENIAL

BROUGHT THIS BOOK

TO FRUITION

TABLE OF CONTENTS

INTRODUCTION

The Jewish holidays are the jewels set in the crown of the months of the year. With their brilliance and radiance they cast a glow on the ordinary days and their recurring regularity. They serve as the wayside palaces that welcome the weary Jewish travellers on their mundane voyage across the monotonous, often stark and uphill highways of life. The holidays relax and uplift the Jews amidst physical and intellectual splendor, and imbue them with religious fervor which helps them carry on until they reach the next holiday-palace.

To get the full value of these holidays, it is important to acquaint oneself with their ceremonies, symbols and significance. For this purpose this book has been written.

Jewish Holidays and Festivals

Jewish Holidays and Festivals

The Sabbath

The first and most important Jewish holiday is the Sabbath, which was given to us on the seventh day of creation. It is also the most frequent holiday, for we celebrate it every Saturday.

Literally, Sabbath means rest. This day is different from the other six days of the week in that it is spent in prayer, religious thought and study in a relaxed and happy atmosphere. The Torah explains that the seventh day is to be a day of rest and cultural growth so that man may be free. If a man has one free day each week, he appreciates freedom and he will remain free at all times. Slaves have no day to call their own.

The Sabbath also reminds us that God created the Universe. As He rested on the seventh day, so does man, His greatest creation, rest on the Sabbath.

Time of Observance

The Sabbath is observed from sundown of the sixth day (Friday), to sundown on the seventh day (Saturday). We begin every Jewish holiday at sundown because the Torah tells us that when God created the world, He considered the evening as the beginning of the day.

Lighting of Sabbath Candles

The Sabbath is welcomed by the lighting of two candles every Friday evening. (In some places one additional candle is lit for each child.) The candles are a symbol of peace, freedom and light which the Sabbath brings to the human soul. They separate the holy seventh day from the six secular days of the week.

The mother, considered by our Sages as the guiding influence of the Jewish family, is privileged to light the candles. She does so also because Eve, the first mother, extinguished the light of eternal life by disobeying God's command not to eat from the tree of knowledge. The present-day mother seeks to repair the wrong done by lighting the candles, and she prays for a long life of happiness and peace.

Kiddush

Kiddush is the blessing recited over wine on the Sabbath and on holidays. The male head of the household chants the kiddush in memory of the first Sabbath of creation and of our deliverance from bondage in Egypt.

Services for Sabbath

Psalms and special poems, *Kabbalath Shabbath* (welcoming the Sabbath), are recited in honor of the Sabbath Queen on Friday evening. *Maariv* (evening prayers) follows. On Saturday morning, *Shacharith* (morning prayers) and *Musaf* (additional prayers) are chanted. Before *Musaf*, a weekly portion of the Torah (Bible) is read. This portion is divided into seven sections. For each section, a man is called to make the blessings over the Torah before and after the reading. The first person called is a *Kohen*, a descendant of Aaron, the brother of Moses and the first high priest. Then a Levite, a descendant of the tribe of Levi, is called. For the remaining sections any Jew can be called. The Kohen and Levite are honored first because they were the spiritual leaders and teachers of the Jews in Egypt and in the Promised Land. *Mincha* (afternoon prayers), the closing service of the Sabbath, is recited before sundown.

THE BEST KNOWN SABBATH PRAYERS AND CHANTS

1. Lechu Nerannena (Come Let Us Sing) The opening prayer in the Friday evening service. A psalm of the Bible, it is a call to worship God, who created the world and all mankind.

2. Lecha Dodi (Come My Beloved) Said on Friday evening; a poem written by Solomon Alkabetz, the Levite, in the 16th century. It welcomes the Sabbath Queen as a bride and declares that the Messiah, from the house of David, will appear in the Holy City of Jerusalem and defeat Israel's enemies.

3. Mizmor Shir L'Yom Hashabbath (A Song for the Sabbath Day) A psalm which praises the justice of the Lord. It was sung in the Temple in Jerusalem on the Sabbath.

4. Veshamru (The Jews Shall Observe the Sabbath) A portion from the Torah commanding the Jews to observe the Sabbath.

5. Vayechulu (And the Heaven and the Earth Were Finished) A portion from the Torah describing how God rested on the seventh day. *Veshamru* and *Vayechulu* are recited every Friday evening.

6. Shalom Aleichem (Peace Be Unto You) When we come

home from the synagogue on Friday night, we chant this famous song welcoming the angels of peace into our homes.

7. (K)EL ADON (Lord of All) Chanted on Sabbath morning; a hymn describing how God created the planets, earth, sun, moon and stars, and set the laws for their continual function.

8. YISMACH MOSHE (Moses Rejoiced) We relate how Moses rejoiced when he was given the Torah.

9. B'RICH SHMEI (Blessed Be the Lord's Name) In this prayer written in Aramaic, we pray to the Lord that we may never have to depend upon Man, but upon God alone. This prayer is said before the open Aron Kodesh (Holy Ark) as we are about to take out the Torah to read the weekly portion.

10. TIKANTAH SHABBATH (Thou Didst Create the Sabbath) We pray for an opportunity to celebrate the Sabbath in Jerusalem. It is chanted in the Musaf service.

11. YISMECHU (They Shall Rejoice) The Sabbath observers shall rejoice in the beauty of the Sabbath and find delight in it. It is also recited during the Musaf service.

12. EIN K'ELOKENU (None Is Like Our Lord) This famous song is very popular with young and old because of its melody and simple repetition of words. It is sung near the end of the Musaf service.

Shalosh Seudoth

Literally, Shalosh Seudoth means "three meals," but it refers to the last and third meal eaten after the Mincha service on the Sabbath. The three meals of Sabbath serve a very important purpose. They strengthen family ties, for the family gathers around the Sabbath table and spends time in eating together, singing songs, and discussing topics of interest. They add festivity and joy to the Sabbath.

Havdalah (*Separation*)

The ceremony of Havdalah takes place immediately at the close of the Sabbath. A long candle is lit in memory of Adam, the first man, who discovered fire. Blessings are made over wine to remind us of the difference between the Sabbath and the rest of the week, and over spices contained in a special decorative box to symbolize a fragrant week. After the Havdalah, it is customary to greet one another with the words, "A Gute Voch," meaning "A Good Week."

M'laveh Malkah (*Farewell to the Queen*)

The Sabbath is considered a queen who has come to us to stay for one day, from Friday at sunset until Saturday night. In honor of her visit, we put on our best clothes and serve our best food. When she is ready to depart, we give her a hearty farewell. We eat a good meal, sing Z'miroth (songs) and discuss Torah subjects.

SPECIAL DISHES AND FOODS OF SABBATH

1. GEFILTE FISH symbolizes the mythical great fish called the Leviathan. Tradition has it that this mythical fish is huge enough to feed permanently all the pious souls in Paradise. Gefilte fish, therefore, is a traditional dish eaten on the Sabbath and other holidays.

2. CHALOTH (twisted breads) are placed on the table on Friday evenings, Saturdays and holidays. At the beginning of the meal a blessing is recited over them, and then they are eaten. They are a symbol of the two measures of Manna, the white substance which fell in the desert and was eaten by the Jews for forty years. The Jews gathered a measure each day and a double measure on Friday, so there would be sufficient for the Sabbath, the day of rest. The two Chaloth, therefore, symbolize rest.

3. CHOLENT originated among the Jews of France. It is a combination of a number of dishes (candied potatoes and prunes, barley and lima beans, peas and barley, meat and potatoes), which are cooked overnight and eaten on the Sabbath. The word comes from the French "chaleur" meaning warmth, and from the Hebrew "shelan" meaning "that which stayed overnight".

4. KUGEL is a round pudding prepared for the Sabbath. It comes from the Hebrew "k'agol," meaning "like a circle," or round. It symbolizes a round, good week.

TRANSLATION OF BLESSINGS FOR SABBATH

FOR LIGHTING CANDLES

Blessed are You, Lord our God, King of the Universe, who has made us holy with His commandments and commanded us to kindle the light of Sabbath.

ON WRAPPING ONESELF IN THE TALITH

Blessed are You, Lord our God, King of the Universe, who has made us holy with His commandments and commanded us to wrap ourselves in the fringed garment.

KIDDUSH FOR SABBATH MORNING

And the children of Israel shall keep the Sabbath, to observe the Sabbath throughout their generations, for an everlasting covenant. It is a sign between Me and the children of Israel forever, that in six days the Lord made the heavens and the earth, and on the seventh day He rested, and ceased His work. Therefore, God blessed the seventh day and made it holy.

Blessed are You, Lord our God, King of the Universe, who creates the fruit of the vine.

FOR BREAD

Blessed are You, Lord our God, King of the Universe, who brings forth bread from the earth.

FOR WINE

Blessed are You, Lord our God, King of the Universe, who creates the fruit of the vine.

SABBATH STORIES

Ariel

About 120 years ago, the Jews of Jerusalem were very poor and often went hungry. The Rabbinical Council of Jerusalem decided to do something to stop the suffering of the Jerusalem Jews. It chose one rabbi to travel to other countries to seek help from other Jewish communities. To travel, years ago, meant to spend many days in desolate places, cross deserts full of wild beasts and risk being attacked by bandits lurking in the darkness of the night. Caravans were well armed, and no man dared to risk his life by traveling alone.

The rabbi chosen by the Council arranged for an Arab caravan leader to take him across the big desert. The rabbi agreed to pay an additional sum of money for stopping in the desert on the Sabbath, in order to enable him to observe his day of rest in the proper manner.

The caravan traveled a whole week. However, when Friday evening came, the leader of the caravan insisted on moving on, in spite of his promise to the rabbi. The Arab gave the rabbi two choices: either to go on with the caravan or to be left behind in one of the most dangerous sections of the desert. Without hesitation, the rabbi chose to stay behind in order not to profane the

Sabbath. In vain did his fellow travelers implore him to go on, as staying behind meant certain death. The rabbi refused.

As the last rays of the sun disappeared over the horizon, the rabbi saw the caravan disappear behind a sand dune. He remained all alone in the vast, limitless stretch of sand. When darkness fell and the stars began to appear in the moonlit sky, the rabbi turned in the direction of Jerusalem and chanted the Friday evening service. He then recited the Kiddush over wine, which he had brought with him, and he sat down to eat his Sabbath meal which consisted of bread and water, chanting the Sabbath Zemiroth, as was his custom. He felt there was nothing to fear, for the Lord would protect him.

However, the rabbi was not alone. A ferocious lion was attracted by the rabbi's Zemiroth and chants. As the rabbi turned, he saw the lion in front of him. He nearly fainted with fright, thinking his end was near. To his surprise, however, the lion stretched out on the sand in front of the rabbi, and his eyes shone with peace and contentment. The rabbi lost all his fear, for he understood that the lion was there to protect him. He continued with his Zemiroth and his after-dinner grace until first the lion and then the rabbi fell asleep.

In the morning, when the rabbi awakened, he saw the lion lying on the sand looking at him with great kindness. He washed, put on his Talith, prayed with fervor and gave thanks to his Creator. The lion watched the swaying rabbi, and his half-closed eyes followed the movements of the Talith. After praying, the rabbi ate the second Sabbath meal, sharing his food with the lion. He studied Torah the rest of the day, chanted the Mincha service and ate the Shalosh Seudoth, and in the late afternoon, after sundown, he chanted the Maariv service and the Havdalah.

As soon as he finished chanting the Havdalah, a change came over the lion. He began to run back and forth, and then stretched out before the rabbi, only to jump up again. This he repeated often until the rabbi understood the lion's intentions. The lion was inviting the rabbi to take a ride on his back. The rabbi climbed on to the lion's back, held on to the lion's mane, and the lion and his passenger were off, in the darkness, to a place known only to the lion. They travelled through the night and as the first rays of the sun appeared over the horizon, the lion approached an oasis.

Upon entering the oasis the rabbi found the caravan, which had left him behind in the desert. His fellow travelers were amazed to see the lion kneel and lie down like a camel. No sooner had the rabbi descended from the lion's back, then the lion arose, stretched his full length, roared, and disappeared in the vastness of the desert. The Arab and the travelers realized then that the rabbi was a pious, holy man and they begged his forgiveness.

Since that day, the rabbi became famous as Rabbi Ariel (Ari means Lion, thus Lion of God). A number of his descendants still live in Jerusalem and are respected as pious and learned people.

(FROM *Jewish Folklore*)

The Treasure

It was a hot Friday night in July. Shmerl the woodcutter woke up in the middle of the night covered with perspiration. The air in the one-room hut where he and his whole family lived was so humid that he could barely catch his breath. He got out of bed, washed his face with cold water and went outdoors to cool off.

It was after midnight and there was not a single person around. Shmerl looked up at the sky and seeing the stars twinkle, he felt that only the Lord and he, Shmerl, were awake in the entire world at that moment. Shmerl was no fool, and being an opportunist, he raised his eyes towards heaven and whispered, "Lord of the Universe, now that every one is asleep and You do not have any problems, perhaps You will have time to listen to me. Please, bless me with one of Your many treasures, and I will be Your servant forever".

No sooner had Shmerl finished his prayer than a small glistening ball began to swirl and dance in front of him, just like a Chanukah dreidl. Shmerl was awestruck, but understood that his prayer had been heard, and his wish was fulfilled. Shmerl stepped up to the ball, but when he tried to touch it, the ball rolled away from him. The faster Shmerl moved toward the ball, the faster the ball rolled away. When Shmerl slowed down, the ball slowed down too. Strangely enough, the distance between Shmerl and the ball always remained exactly the same. Shmerl was puzzled, but he felt that the ball was his treasure, and he would not let it slip away from him. The ball kept on rolling and Shmerl kept on following it.

Soon he realized that he had left the town, and was crossing the fields and meadows, but still the distance between him and the ball had not changed one bit. Sometimes a hidden voice seemed to say to him, "Hurry, Shmerl, and throw your robe over the treasure, and then it will be yours." Shmerl realized that this could only be the voice of Satan who wanted him to commit a sin on the Sabbath. For to pick up the treasure and carry it home would create a commotion there. His wife would tell the neighbors, the whole town would gather in front of his home instead of attending services in the Shul, and that would cause Jews to profane the Sabbath. Shmerl slowed his pace; no one would make him profane the Sabbath and be a bad example to others. The ball also slowed its pace.

While following the rolling treasure Shmerl thought: "If I could only get hold of the treasure without profaning the Sabbath, it would be so good. In my old age, I would not have to work so hard any more, and I would buy fine clothes for my faithful wife, who has worked so hard all her life and cannot afford a new dress. I would give my children the best education possible, so they would not have to be ignorant, as I am. I would buy a house with three rooms and not have to live in a one-room hut, especially during the hot summer days. Maybe it would not be such a great sin to grab the treasure now, and then give charity to atone for this little sin. Of course, I would do it only for the sake of my wife and my poor children, but . . . these are only Satanic thoughts. If I am worthy of the treasure, I'll get it the right way!"

Shmerl raised his eyes to heaven and said: "Master of the World, whom are you teasing? Are you teasing me, Shmerl the woodcutter? If you want to give me a treasure, please give it to me, but don't play tricks on me."

Suddenly, Shmerl noticed that he was already approaching the next village. He had walked a long distance, and in anger, he turned back towards his home.

"I will not follow you any more," he said to the ball. "The Lord does not make fun of people. Satan must have overheard my prayer and has been trying to tease me."

As he turned back, the glistening ball jumped ahead of him and again began to roll back toward his home town, keeping the same distance as before.

"I won't tell anybody about this incident," Shmerl thought. "Most people won't believe me, and some will laugh at me. I won't even tell my wife. She may get angry with me and call me Shlumiel, Good-for-nothing." I had one good chance in my lifetime and missed it. My Creator and I know about it, and that is enough for me. Anyhow, why should I get excited about a treasure? What is money? Nothing. It is just an instrument of sin, murder and cheating. I am better off without the treasure."

Shmerl was approaching his hut. The door was still open as he had left it. The ball rolled ahead of him through the door, into the hut, and right under the bed. Shmerl took his robe and threw it over the swirling ball. Quietly he got into bed, but could not sleep. And again he resolved not to tell anybody about his experience until after sundown.

Because Shmerl showed strength of character and did not profane the Sabbath, the treasure remained under his bed. He found it after he had chanted the Havdalah, but instead of the ball, he found a sack full of gold. Shmerl became the richest man in town. Yet his wife complained from time to time.

"What kind of a man did I marry, a man with a heart of stone? A whole day long he hid a treasure under his bed without uttering a word, without betraying his emotions to me, his devoted wife. And maybe," she added with a hurt look, "the treasure did not disappear during the day because of my prayers mixed with tears, and not because of my stone-hearted husband's particular virtues."

Shmerl, feeling guilty, tried to pacify her: "I am sure that only your prayers kept the treasure in place. I only brought it to your home." And then they would look at each other, and the smiles on their faces would show the deep love and devotion they felt.

(I. L. PERETZ)

SABBATH QUESTIONS

True or False

Sabbath means rest.

Sabbath or any holiday is observed from sundown to sundown.

Musaf comes before Shacharith.

L'cha Dodi is chanted at Mincha service.

Three men are called to the Torah on Sabbath.

M'lave Malka is a prayer.

Shalosh Seudoth is a holiday.

Havdalah is performed on Saturday night.

Kiddush is recited on Friday evening.

Draw a Line Under the Correct Answer

Yom Tov is: a good day, a fast day, a rainy day.

Sabbath begins at sundown, morning, midnight.

Kiddush is a chant over wine, a prayer for the dead, blessing over herbs.

Kohen is a priest, prince, cantor.

Mincha is a service in the afternoon, morning, evening.

Maariv is a service, in the afternoon, morning, evening.

Shacharith is a service in the afternoon, morning, evening.

Musaf is a service in the afternoon, morning, evening.

Shalom Aleichem is a chant, the name of a writer, a Hebrew greeting.

Why

Why do we observe Sabbath every seventh day?

Why do we light candles?

Why do we make Kiddush?

Why do we use Chaloth?

Why do we read a portion of the Torah and Prophets each Sabbath?

Why do we make Havdalah?

When

When do we observe the Sabbath?

Light candles?

Chant Kiddush?

Chant Kabbalath Shabbath?

Observe Shalosh Seudoth?

Eat Cholent, Kugel, Gefilte fish?

Who Are the Following

A rabbi, a gabbai, a chazan, a baal koreh, kohen, levi, Israelite?

General Questions

How do you observe the Sabbath?

Why do you think that Sabbath is so important to Jewish life?

Do you like the observance of Sabbath and why?

How do you connect Israel with the Sabbath?

How do you participate in Sabbath services?

How do you make Sabbath enjoyable and pleasant?

What does Sabbath mean literally and spiritually?

Rosh Hashanah

(THE JEWISH NEW YEAR)

Rosh Hashanah means the head or beginning of the Jewish year. It is the birthday of the world, for tradition tells us that the world was created then.

Rosh Hashanah is the day when God judges each man according to his deeds—good and bad. It is therefore also known as "Yom Hazikaron," the Day of Remembrance, and "Yom Hadin," the Day of Judgment.

Rosh Hashanah is also known as "Yom Teruah," the day of the blowing of the Shofar (ram's horn), which is blown to remind us to repent for our sins, because this is the day of judgment. The use of the Shofar goes back to the time of our ancestors when Abraham was willing to sacrifice his only son Isaac, when God

27

told him to do so, in order to test Abraham. At the last moment, the Almighty commanded Abraham to substitute the ram for Isaac. By blowing the horn, we seek to recall Abraham's complete faith in the Lord.

Time of Observance

Rosh Hashanah is observed for two days. It comes on the first and second days of the Hebrew month of Tishri (usually in September), which is the first month of the Hebrew calendar. Like the Sabbath, it begins on the evening before the first day, with the lighting of candles, and ends at nightfall of the second day.

Rosh Hashanah Greetings

On Rosh Hashanah, as judgment day, the decision of the Lord concerning the lot of each Jew is noted in special symbolic books. Every righteous Jew has his name entered in the Book of Life immediately. Therefore, upon leaving the synagogue after the Maariv service, on the eve of Rosh Hashanah, as well as on meeting a friend on either day of the holiday, the greeting is, "L'Shanah Tova Tikasevu," which means, "May you be inscribed in the Book of Life for the next year."

Selichoth

The High Holy Days begin with the special services known as *Selichoth*, prayers asking forgiveness (from the Hebrew "Slicha" meaning forgiveness). These *Selichoth* are usually chanted after midnight, beginning a week before Rosh Hashanah, and continuing to Yom Kippur. They are said after midnight to show our sincerity and our readiness to sacrifice sleep for forgiveness.

The Ten Days of Repentance

The ten days beginning with the first day of Rosh Hashanah and ending with Yom Kippur, are called the "Ten Days of Repentance." During these days, we regret our sins, ask God's forgiveness, and resolve to mend our ways during the coming year.

Fast of Gedaliah

After the destruction of the First Jewish Temple in Jerusalem, Nebuchadnezzar, the conquering king of Babylon, appointed a Jewish governor for Judea. This governor was called Gedaliah. As long as Gedaliah was governor, the Jews hoped that they would soon regain their rights and their independence. Unfortunately, the Egyptians conspired to have Gedaliah murdered. The Jews in Jerusalem then fled, and with them went, for a long time, the Jewish cultural center in Israel. The whole course of Jewish history might well have been different had Gedaliah lived. In remembrance of the death of Gedaliah, a fast day is observed on the day following Rosh Hashanah, or the third day of Tishri.

THE BEST KNOWN ROSH HASHANAH PRAYERS

Since Rosh Hashanah is the day of judgment, the prayers stress the greatness and everlastingness of the Lord who is the Judge.

1. ZOCHREINU L'CHAIM (Remember Us to Life) A prayer said at each of the seven services of Rosh Hashanah, requesting the Lord to remember us and inscribe us in the Book of Life.

2. HASHEM MELECH (The Lord Is King) This prayer, said at the morning and Musaf services on Rosh Hashanah, declares that the Lord is, was, and will be, King of the universe.

3. L'EL ORECH DIN (To the Lord Who Sits in Judgment) A prayer arranged alphabetically, which describes the way the Lord judges mankind on Rosh Hashanah.

4. AVINU MALKENU (Our Father, Our King) This prayer lists many requests that we ask of the Lord for the New Year.
5. UNESANEH TOKEF (Let Us Tell How Holy Is This Day) This prayer said both days of Rosh Hashanah at the morning service, describes how all get ready for judgment on Rosh Hashanah, and how the Lord decides what shall be each one's fate during the coming year.
6. VECHOL MAAMINIM (Everyone Believes) This prayer describes God's power, kindness, and readiness to forgive.

The Torah Readings on Rosh Hashanah

On each of the two days of Rosh Hashanah, portions of the Bible are read between Shacharith (morning prayer) and Musaf. On the first day, that part of the Book B'reshith is read which tells of the birth of Isaac, and of Ishmael's leaving Abraham's house. The reading from the Early Prophets describes the birth of Samuel and his training for prophecy in the home of the High Priest Eli.

The reading from the Torah on the second day of Rosh Hashanah tells about the readiness of Abraham to sacrifice his only son, Isaac, when the Lord, in order to test him, orders him to do so. At the last moment, Abraham is told to sacrifice a ram instead of Isaac.

SPECIAL ROSH HASHANAH CUSTOMS

TASHLICH   In the afternoon of Rosh Hashanah, prayers are said at a river or any other body of running water. There we symbolically throw away our sins which are carried off by the running water.

SPECIAL FOODS   We eat round Challah, honey, and new fruits, to symbolize the hope that the coming year will be round, smooth and sweet. We say a special blessing, "Shehecheyanu," to thank God for keeping us alive this far.

We also eat *Tzimes* which is a dish made from carrots. The Yiddish word for carrots is "Meyrin" which means to increase. Therefore, we eat Tzimes on Rosh Hashanah as a symbol that God will increase our privileges.

TRANSLATION OF BLESSINGS FOR ROSH HASHANAH

FOR LIGHTING CANDLES

Blessed are You, Lord our God, King of the Universe, who sanctified us with His commandments and commanded us to light the candle of the festival.

Blessed are You, Lord our God, King of the Universe, who has kept us alive and preserved us, and enabled us to reach this present time.

ROSH HASHANAH GREETING

You shall be inscribed in the Book of Life for a happy year.

FOR A NEW FRUIT

Blessed are You, Lord our God, King of the Universe, creator of the fruit of the tree.

Blessed are You, Lord our God, King of the Universe, who has kept us alive and preserved us, and enabled us to reach this present time.

FOR HONEY

May it be the will of God to grant us a sweet and good New Year.

FOR WINE

Blessed are You, Lord our God, King of the Universe, creator of the fruit of the vine.

FOR TALITH

Blessed are You, Lord our God, King of the Universe, who has sanctified us with his commandments, and commanded us to wrap ourselves in the fringed garment.

ROSH HASHANAH FOLKLORE

Rabbi Amnon

In the city of Mayence, there lived a famous rabbi by the name of Rabbi Amnon whom the King respected and liked. But the King had an advisor who was jealous of Rabbi Amnon and tried to get rid of him. He kept on telling the King that he should force Rabbi Amnon to become a Christian.

One day, the King weakened and ordered Rabbi Amnon to accept Christianity. Rabbi Amnon asked for three days to think it over. The King granted Rabbi Amnon's request, thinking that the rabbi would then accept Christianity.

After the three days passed, Rabbi Amnon refused to come to the King, because he knew what awaited him when he refused to accept Christianity. The King was very angry that the rabbi had disobeyed him, and he ordered Rabbi Amnon to be brought before him. The King asked, "Why did you not come to give me the answer after three days?" Rabbi Amnon answered, "Because I did not want to accept Christianity." The King said, "Because you have refused to obey the order, you shall be severely punished. Your feet, which refused to carry you, shall be cut off." The guards obeyed the King's command. It happened to be Rosh Hashanah, and the bleeding rabbi asked to be brought to the synagogue. He asked to be permitted to say a prayer. Then he composed and recited the famous prayer, "Unesaneh Tokef," and when he had finished it, he died in the synagogue.

In honor of the martyred rabbi, and because the prayer describes how the Lord judges everyone on the High Holy Days, it is the custom to chant this prayer on Rosh Hashanah and on Yom Kippur in every synagogue and temple all over the world.

The Tzadik of Nemirov

Every year during Selichoth time, the Tzadik (Holy Rabbi) of Nemirov disappeared. His family came to Shul during the midnight service of Selichoth, but the Tzadik could not be found either in the Shul or at his home. He simply disappeared.

When non-believers chided the rabbi's followers concerning his disappearance, his followers insisted that the rabbi went to heaven to defend and plead for poor Jews accused by Satan of doing wrong. In heaven, the rabbi was able to challenge Satan directly before the Master of the world, they said.

Once a Jew, not a follower of the Tzadik, visited the synagogue on Selichoth night. Upon being told about the disappearance of the rabbi, he decided to investigate the whole thing.

The Jew stole into the rabbi's bedroom and hid himself under the rabbi's bed. When midnight came, he heard the family get up, dress and leave for the synagogue. The rabbi did not move. When silence reigned in his home, the rabbi, moaning and groaning, got up from his bed, and to the Jew's consternation, dressed in the clothes of a Russian peasant, smeared his face with soot so as not to be recognized, took a heavy ax and left the house. The Jew followed with a question in his mind: "He may be a rabbi in the day time and a bandit during the night."

The rabbi walked in the shadows of the houses so as not to be seen, until he had left the town and entered a forest. The Jew was very frightened, but his curiosity got the best of him and he followed the rabbi deep into the forest. At one place, the rabbi stopped, took his ax and cut down a tree. He then chopped it into smaller pieces, tied them in a bundle, and went on. He finally came to a clearing in the forest. The Jew saw the rabbi approach a small hut in the clearance, and knock at the door. A woman's weak voice asked. "Who is there?"

"This is Vasil, the peasant," the rabbi answered in Russian.

"What do you want, Vasil?"

"I brought you some wood because you are sick."

"But how much will it cost me?"

"Six kopecks."

"But I do not have the money, nor do I know when I will have it."

The rabbi got angry. In a gruff and scolding voice, he said to her, "I, a plain Russian peasant, am willing to trust you with six kopecks, but you, who have such a great Lord in heaven, do not want to trust in Him for six kopecks. You ought to be ashamed of yourself."

Slowly, a weak hand opened the door and let the rabbi in. The Jew ran to the window and looked inside. He saw the rabbi light the stove, and then heat some water, make tea, and give it to the woman, who was sick and cold. While doing this, he chanted the Selichoth in a low voice. . . .

The Jew thereafter became one of the staunchest supporters and followers of the Rabbi. Upon hearing people tell about the Tzadik of Nemirov going to heaven to intercede for the poor people, he would add:

"Who knows?"—if not even higher than that."

(I. L. PERETZ)

ROSH HASHANAH QUESTIONS

True or False

Rosh Hashanah means the holiday of fruit.

Rosh Hashanah is observed on the first and second days of Tishri.

Tashlich is a ceremony of symbolically throwing away our sins.

The Ten Days of Repentance begin with Rosh Hashanah and end with Yom Kippur.

Selichoth are books.

Shehecheyanu is a blessing.

Fast of Gedaliah is observed on Rosh Hashanah.

L'Shanah Tova Tikasevu means: "May you be inscribed in the Book of Life for the next year."

Draw a Line Under the Correct Answer

Rosh Hashanah means: head of the tribe, head of the year, head of the month.

Selichoth are: branches of trees, prayers, books.

Tashlich means: ceremony over wine, casting sins in water, thanksgiving.

Shehechyanu is: A blessing of thanksgiving, for fruit, for bread.

Gedaliah was killed because: the Jews did not like him, the Egyptians did not like him, the Babylonians did not like him.

A Machzor is: a holiday prayer book, a daily prayer book, a science book.

Why

Why do we blow the Shofar on Rosh Hashanah?

Eat a round Challah?

Chant the blessing Shehecheyanu?

Eat honey?

Call Rosh Hashanah: Yom Hazikaron, Yom Hadin, Yom Teruah?

General Questions

What kind of a calendar do we Jews use?

Could you mention the names of the months in the Jewish calendar?

Why is Rosh Hashanah observed on the first two days of Tishri?

Why should a Jew observe Rosh Hashanah?

How do you observe Rosh Hashanah?

How could Rosh Hashanah observance help you in your future life?

Do you make it a practice to greet every person every day?

Do you make it a practice to greet people with L'Shanah Tovah on Rosh Hashanah?

Why are greetings so important in everyone's life?

Yom Kippur

Yom Kippur (The Day of Forgiveness or Atonement) comes on the tenth day of the Jewish month of Tishri (September or October). It is the last of the Ten Days of Repentance, and is the most solemn day of the Jewish calendar. It is believed that those who have not been good enough to be written into the Book of Life immediately on Rosh Hashanah, are given ten days to repent, pray for forgiveness, and do good deeds until Yom Kippur, when their fate will be decided. The entire day of Forgiveness (Yom Kippur) is spent in fasting and praying.

Time of Observance

Yom Kippur is observed from before sundown on the ninth day of the Hebrew month of Tishri to sundown on the tenth day

37

of the Hebrew month of Tishri. The supper meal is eaten before sundown. Then the mother lights the candles with a special blessing for Yom Kippur. The father blesses mother and each child before going to the synagogue.

Services for Yom Kippur

The opening service of Yom Kippur evening is the traditional Kol Nidre which is followed by the Maariv service. The next morning, the Shacharith Service is said, followed by the reading of the Torah portion. Then the Musaf service is chanted. Late in the afternoon, the Mincha service is said, followed by the closing Yom Kippur service called Neilah. At the end of Neilah, the Shofar is blown to signify the end of Yom Kippur.

THE BEST KNOWN YOM KIPPUR PRAYERS

1. KOL NIDRE (All Vows) is recited before sundown on the eve of Yom Kippur. The cantor chants this prayer while surrounded by the elders of the congregation, who hold Torah scrolls. Kol Nidre is a declaration that all promises made by man to God and to himself during the next year, which he will not be able to keep, shall be null and void. However, vows and promises made by anyone to his fellow man are not cancelled by the Kol Nidre declaration.
2. SHEMA KOLENU (Hear Our Cry) This prayer is recited toward the end of each service on Yom Kippur. In it we ask the Lord to have mercy on us, accept our prayers and always be with us.
3. AL CHET (For the Sin) This prayer also is recited toward the end of each service on Yom Kippur. In it we list the sins for which we ask the Lord's forgiveness.
4. ALENU LESHABEACH (It Is Our Duty to Praise) This prayer which concludes the three daily services throughout the year has a special place in the Musaf service of Yom Kippur. When

the cantor repeats aloud this prayer he kneels to the floor when he proclaims the Lord as the King of Kings, the Holy One Blessed Be He. He is then helped to his feet to continue the service.

5. KEE ANU AMECHA (For We Are Your People) This too is repeated in every one of the services of Yom Kippur. We ask the Lord to forgive our sins because we are His people and children and He is our God and Father.

6. NEILAH (Closing) This is the closing or final service of Yom Kippur. It is the Jewish belief that the gates of heaven are open during the Days of Repentance to receive our prayers for forgiveness and that they close after the Neilah service. The Neilah service is very beautiful, and the Jews stand throughout the service. They pray that the good lot which they hope has been assigned to them earlier, should receive the final seal of approval at the Neilah service.

Torah Readings for Yom Kippur

The Torah is read twice on Yom Kippur day, once after the Shacharith service and again at the Mincha service. In the morning we read that portion of the book of Leviticus which describes the service conducted by the High Priest in the Temple on Yom Kippur.

At the Mincha service we read the portion of Leviticus which tells us which relatives one can or cannot marry. This portion cautions us not to do the immoral things that the former inhabitants of the Land of Israel did, if we wish to remain in the land. We also read about the prophet Jonah, who was sent to tell Nineveh, the wicked city of Assyria, that it was to be destroyed because it was full of sin. Jonah ran away on a boat in order not to preach to Nineveh. A storm arose and he was thrown overboard by his fellow travellers, when they found out that he was running away from the Lord. A whale swallowed him and brought him back. Jonah then realized that there is no escape from God and he did as he was told. This is read on Yom Kippur in order to bring home to the Jews that God is everywhere.

YOM KIPPUR FOLKLORE

Rabbi Salanter and Kol Nidre

Once there was a great rabbi by the name of Rabbi Israel Salanter. On one Yom Kippur eve, when the whole congregation was waiting in the synagogue for their rabbi to chant the Kol Nidre, as they would not start the service without him, the rabbi did not arrive. They waited and waited and finally sent a messenger to the rabbi's house, but the rabbi was not home either. They could not understand where the rabbi had disappeared. Finally, after two hours of waiting and searching for the rabbi, they saw him entering the synagogue. When asked for an explanation, the much revered rabbi explained, "When I was walking to the synagogue this evening, I passed a house where a little child was crying. It seems that the mother went to the synagogue and left the child sleeping. So I went into the house and took care of the baby until he fell asleep, as I believe that a crying baby is more important than the chanting of Kol Nidre on time."

The Tzadik

During the Neilah, or closing, service of Yom Kippur, a great Hasidic Rabbi was standing in the pulpit, chanting the prayers in his role of Shliach Tzibur, or messenger of the congregation, since who was worthier than he of being the Shliach Tzibur? Suddenly, the rabbi stopped chanting as if he were paralyzed—his body shook but not a sound came from his throat. The people were puzzled. Minutes passed by, half an hour passed, an hour passed, and still there was no sound. It was late in the day and the people in the synagague were anxious to go home to break their fast, but they did not move from their seats, and complete silence reigned in the synagogue. The adherents of the holy man suspected that the rabbi was in communication with God and, therefore, must not be disturbed.

In the meantime, Yosel, the eight-year-old son of a farmer who had come to the village to pray, came to the synagogue to wait for Yom Kippur to come to an end and walk home with his father. As Yosel arrived at the entrance of the synagogue, he was overwhelmed by the complete silence. He saw all the people standing silently and staring at the great rabbi. Yosel stood awed by the sight, and quite suddenly, he felt like praying to God. The urge to pray became stronger and stronger by the minute; he *must* express himself. Since Yosel lived on a farm and had not been given the opportunity of learning the prayers in Hebrew, the only way he knew of expressing his joys and sorrows was by whistling.

Suddenly, the entire congregation heard a piercing whistle at the door of the synagogue. Many hurried to find the culprit who had dared do such a thing while the rabbi was in communication with God. But the holy man, as if coming to life suddenly, asked, "Where is the great Tzadik who whistled from the depths of his heart and pierced the gates of heaven, and thus caused God to nullify the severe decree?" But the Tzadik could not be found anywhere.

(J. L. PERETZ)

YOM KIPPUR QUESTIONS

True or False

Yom Kippur is the Day of Atonement.
Yom Kippur is the first day of the Ten Days of Repentance.
Kol Nidre is a declaration.
Kol Nidre nullifies all promises of man to man.
Jonah was a prophet.
We eat Cholent on Yom Kippur.
We pray a whole day on Yom Kippur.

Draw a Line Under the Correct Answer

We chant Kol Nidre on: Passover, Yom Kippur, Rosh Hashanah.
The Marranos were: Spanish Jews, German Jews, Polish Jews.
Neilah is: the first service, second service, last service.
Jonah was: a merchant, a king, a prophet.
Nineveh was: in Assyria, Syria, Persia.
We blow the Shofar: after Kol Nidre, after Musaf, after Neilah.

Why

Why do we chant the Kol Nidre?
Why do we read the chapter about Jonah and the whale?
Why do we fast?
Why is it important to keep a promise?

General Questions

What is the difference between Rosh Hashanah and Yom Kippur?
Why is Yom Kippur so important?
Which promises does Kol Nidre nullify, and which does it not
   nullify?
Do you know of any instance when a broken promise hurt some-
   one?

Sukkoth

HOSHANAH RABBAH, SHEMINI ATZERETH,
SIMCHATH TORAH

The holiday of Sukkoth is celebrated from the 15th through the 22nd day of Tishri (September or October). It includes three other holiday celebrations: Hoshanah Rabbah, Shemini Atzereth and Simchath Torah.

Sukkoth means "huts." When the Jews lived in the desert after their exodus from Egypt, they gathered and dwelt in huts and tents. Later, when they settled in Israel, they again used small huts during harvest time. These field huts served as temporary dwellings to save valuable time and energy for the Jewish farmers. We therefore call this holiday the "Holiday of Huts"

(Chag Hasukkoth), as well as the "Holiday of Ingathering" (Chag Heasif).

SPECIAL SUKKOTH CUSTOMS

We observe the Holiday of Huts today by erecting temporary huts, and eating in the Sukkoth during the holiday. The Sukkah (hut) represents the faith our ancestors had in the Lord, that he would take them across the dangerous desert in safety. When we sit in a Sukkah, we express our faith in and reliance on God.

Because it is also a harvest festival and an agricultural holiday, we use the following four plants: the Ethrog, Lulav, Hadas and Aravah.

1. *Ethrog:* The Ethrog is a citron fruit which grows all year on its tree, and has a good smell and a good taste. It symbolizes those individuals who are both educated and who do good deeds.

2. *Lulav:* The Lulav is a branch of a palm tree which produces good fruit, but has no odor. It represents people with great wealth, but without good deeds.

3. *Hadas:* The Hadas is a myrtle branch. It has a pleasant odor but no taste. It is used as a symbol for those people who are educated, but who do not use their knowledge for the benefit of the welfare of their fellow men.

4. *Aravah:* The Aravah is a willow branch. It can neither be eaten, nor does it have a good smell. It represents people without education, without money, and without good deeds.

The Lulav is bound together with three myrtles and two willows. Then the Ethrog is held in the left hand, while the Lulav, the myrtles and willows are held in the right hand near the ethrog, and the blessing is chanted over the four plants. This denotes the unity of the different kinds of people represented by these plants.

The four plants are also used during the Sukkoth holiday in making a Hakafa (circuit) around the congregation standing in the synagogue. The cantor leads the procession, and each man who has a Lulav and Ethrog follows behind him. During the procession, the cantor recites the Hoshanah prayers, asking for blessings on the land and fruit of Israel.

Hoshanah Rabbah

Hoshanah Rabbah, or the great deliverance day, is observed on the seventh day of Sukkoth. In addition to a special service, there take place seven Hakafoth (circuits) around the synagogue. On this day also, a bunch of willow branches, or Hoshanoth, are used with our prayers. As we say a certain prayer, we beat the willow branches against the synagogue benches, to cause the leaves to fall off. This represents:

1. A symbol of the renewal of life—old leaves fall off in the fall season and new ones grow in the spring season; old generations pass on and are replaced by new generations.

2. A reminder of the Babylonian captivity. When the Jews were exiled to Babylon, after the destruction of the First Temple (586 B.C.E.*), they were commanded by their captors to entertain them by playing happy songs. Instead, the Jews hung their instruments on willow branches and refused to play while their Temple was being destroyed.

3. It is believed that on Hoshanah Rabbah, God delivers his final decision as to the fate of each person for the forthcoming year.

Shemini Atzereth

The eighth day of Sukkoth is called Shemini Atzereth (eighth day of the holiday). On that day we pray for rain in Israel. Since Israel is an agricultural country with a scarcity of water, by praying for rain we show our solidarity with the Jews of Israel. On Shemini Atzereth, we also say a special prayer in commemoration

* Before the Common Era

of our dear departed, the same as we do on Yom Kippur, the last day of Passover, and the second day of Shavuoth. This prayer is called Yizkor.

Simchath Torah

Simchath Torah, or Rejoicing with the Torah, is celebrated on the 23rd day of Tishri, or the day following Shemini Atzereth. On that day, Jews circle about in the synagogue seven or more times while holding the scrolls of the Torah. This circling is called in Hebrew "Hakafoth." Children carry flags with suitable inscriptions and all sing and dance, rejoicing in our great inheritance. Before the Hakafoth, special portions of the Torah, called the "Atah Haretah," are read by assigned people who consider it a great honor to be so privileged.

On Simchath Torah the reading of the last chapters in the last book of the Torah is completed and the reading of the first book is begun immediately. This signifies that the Torah has no beginning and no end.

We rejoice in completing it as well as in beginning it again. Every man and boy who has been Bar Mitzvah is called to make a blessing over the Torah. On Simchath Torah, even the small children who are not as yet Bar Mitzvah are honored by being called upon to make the blessing together over the Torah.

TRANSLATION OF BLESSINGS FOR SUKKOTH

FOR LIGHTING CANDLES

Blessed are You, Lord our God, King of the Universe, who has sanctified us with His commandments and commanded us to light the festival candle.

Blessed are You, Lord our God, King of the Universe, who has kept us alive, preserved us, and enabled us to reach this present time.

FOR TALITH

Blessed are You, Lord our God, King of the Universe, who has sanctified us with His commandments and commanded us to wrap ourselves in the fringed garment.

FOR THE SUKKAH

Blessed are You, Lord our God, King of the Universe, who has sanctified us with His commandments and commanded us to sit in a sukkah.

FOR ETHROG AND LULAV

Blessed are You, Lord our God, King of the Universe, who sanctified us with His commandments and commanded us to take the Lulav.

FOR WINE

Blessed are You, Lord our God, King of the Universe, creator of the fruit of the vine.

FOR CHALLAH

Blessed are You, Lord our God, King of the Universe, who brings forth bread from the earth.

SUKKOTH STORIES

The Most Valuable Merchandise

A great sage once traveled by boat across the ocean in the company of many rich merchants. During the journey, the merchants continually boasted about the beauty and quality of their particular type of merchandise. The sage, not to be outdone, also boasted about his merchandise and praised it very highly, but refused to reveal what it was. During the voyage, the ship was attacked by pirates who seized all the valuable merchandise they could find. However, they could find nothing that belonged to the great sage.

When the ship came to port, the townspeople gathered to welcome the sage, and honored him by offering him the position of rabbi. In time, he became very wealthy but never forgot his fellow travelers, the merchants, who had lost all their possessions to the pirates. "You see," the sage would say, "my merchandise was the Torah, which could not be stolen from me, and which proved to be the best merchandise of all."

Abbah Hilkiah

Abbah Hilkiah was the grandson of Honi Hamaagal, and like his great ancestor, he also could bring rain by praying to God.

Once, when there was a drought in the land of Israel, two sages came to him to ask him to pray to God for rain. Abbah Hilkiah was then working in his field. He paid no attention to the two men.

Towards evening, he placed his bundle of wood on one shoulder, his robe on the other shoulder, and his shoes he held in his hand. When he had to cross a stream he put them on. When he passed through thorns, he raised his garments. His wife came out to greet him upon his return. When they reached the entrance of his house, his wife entered first, he second, and the sages last. The sages sat down at a table, wondering at the peculiar behavior of Abbah, as he did not invite them to eat with him. Abbah broke bread, gave one portion to his older son and two parts to his younger son.

When Abbah finished his meal he told his wife, "Let us go up to the attic, I have something important to tell you." The sages, left alone, wondered all the more at this strange conduct.

When Abbah reached the attic he said to his wife, "Let us both pray to God for rain, here in the attic, so that the sages will not know that rain came because of our prayers, and they will not need to thank us." Abbah prayed in one corner and his wife in another. Rain came as soon as they had finished. Abbah then came down and asked the visitors, "May I know the reason for your visit?"

"We came to ask you to pray for rain," answered the sages.

"But the rain came down without my help," said Abbah.

However, the sages knew that the rain came because Abbah and his wife had prayed to God and they said, "We know that because of you the rain came, but before we leave, would you be kind enough to explain a few things?" Abbah agreed to satisfy their curiosity. "Why did you refuse to answer our greeting in the field?" the sages asked. "Because I am a hired laborer and did not want to waste my employer's time."

"Why did you put a bundle of wood on one shoulder and the robe on another?" they continued.

"The robe I borrowed and did not want to ruin it by putting wood on it."

"Why did you put on your shoes only when you reached a stream?"

"Walking on the road I could see the ground, but walking on the bottom of a stream there might be something that would hurt my feet."

"Why did you not invite us to break bread with you?"

"Because I have very little of it, and did not want to extend a false invitation to you."

"Why did you give the older son one portion of bread and two portions to your younger son?"

"Because the older one stays home, but the younger goes to school to study all day long."

"Why did the first rain cloud appear from the direction where your wife stood?"

"Because my wife gives bread to the poor and her help is direct, while I give money for charity, which is not direct help. Also, when our neighbors annoyed us, I prayed to God to remove them from our neighborhood, while my wife prayed to change their bad hearts into good ones. God listened to her prayer and we now have excellent neighbors."

The sages understood why God considered Abbah Hilkiah so great as to comply with his prayers.

QUESTIONS FOR SUKKOTH, SHEMINI ATZERETH, SIMCHATH TORAH

True or False

Sukkoth is the Jewish Arbor Day.
Sukkoth is the Jewish Thanksgiving Day.
Sukkoth commemorates the exodus from Egypt.
Sukkoth means "huts."
Sukkoth is in the month of Nissan.
Hoshanah Rabbah is the 8th day of Sukkoth.
Shemini Atzereth is the 8th day of Sukkoth.
On Simchath Torah we make Hakafoth (rounds).
Atah Haretah is a blessing.
We eat in sukkoth seven days.

Why

Why do we eat in sukkoth on the Sukkoth holiday?
Why do we call Sukkoth the holiday of Ingathering?
Why do we rejoice on Simchath Torah?
Why do we make a joint blessing over the Lulav, Ethrog, Aravah and Hadas?

When

When do we celebrate Sukkoth?
When do we celebrate Hoshanah Rabbah?
When do we celebrate Shemini Atzereth?
When do we chant a special prayer for rain?
When do we celebrate Simchath Torah?

What Are the Following

Hakafoth, Atah Haretah, Hoshanoth, sukkoth, Lulav, Aravim, Hadas, Ethrog, Chag Heasif, Tishri?

General Questions

Why is Sukkoth so important to the Jews of Israel and to the Jews all over the world?

Why should we Jews constantly think about the land of Israel?

Why is Israel important to the Jews of the world?

Why are the Jews of the world important to Israel?

Could you show some connection between each holiday in the Jewish calendar and the land of Israel?

How do you observe Sukkoth, Simchath Torah?

Chanukah

The holiday of Chanukah is celebrated for eight days from the 25th day of the Hebrew month of Kislev (December) to the second day of the Hebrew month of Teveth (December). Chanukah celebrates the victory of the Jews over the Greeks in the time of the Second Temple, and the regaining of Jewish independence and the right to practice the Jewish religion. This holiday has two names—Chanukah, and the Holiday of Lights. The word Chanukah can be divided into two Hebrew words:

Chanu means they rested;

Kah in Hebrew numbers equals 25.

The Jews rested on the 25th day of Kislev from their battles against the Greeks.

It is called the Holiday of Lights because the Temple lamp was lit in Jerusalem for eight days, and this we do also during our celebration of this holiday.

The Story of Chanukah

In 160 B.C.E., the Jews lived in Palestine and the Second Temple stood in Jerusalem. The Jews were ruled at that time by Syrian Greek King Antiochus. He tried to force the Jews to stop believing in their God, to change their traditions and customs, and worship the many gods of the Greeks. The Jews refused, and rebelled against him. The revolt was led by the eighty-year-old Kohen (priest) Mattathias, the Hasmonean, and his five brave sons. Mattathias died soon after the beginning of the revolt, and his son Judah the Maccabee (the Hammer) became the leader. He defeated the Greeks in many battles, then drove them out of Judea, and once more the Jews were free in their own land.

The first wish of the Jews then was to relight the Menorah in the Temple in Jerusalem. To do this, they needed pure oil especially prepared for this purpose.

They first cleaned up the Temple which had been neglected and made unclean by the Greeks during the war. Then they searched for the oil necessary to light the Menorah. They found only a small jug of oil which bore the seal of the Kohen Gadol (High Priest), stating that it was pure. The oil in the jug was enough, however, for only one day, and it would take eight days to make pure oil. The Menorah was lit with this small amount of oil, and miraculously remained lit for eight days. In memory of this miracle, we light candles each year for the eight days of Chanukah.

HEROES OF CHANUKAH

1. MATTATHIAS The old priest who started the revolt against the Greeks.

2. JUDAH THE MACCABEE (the Hammer) One of the five sons of

Mattathias, who became the leader of the Jews after Mattathias died, and drove the Greeks out of Judea. Judah was also called the "Maccabee" because on his battle flag were the letters M-K-B-Y, an abbreviation of the Hebrew words Mi-Kamocha-Baelim-Adoshem, meaning "Who is like Thee among the gods, oh Lord?"

3. ELIEZER   A priest who was killed by the Greeks because he refused to eat non-kosher food.

4. HANNAH   Her seven sons were killed by the cruel King Antiochus, because they refused to bow down before a Greek idol.

CUSTOMS AND PRACTICES OF CHANUKAH

1. We light Chanukah candles for eight days. We light the first candle on the evening of the 24th day of Kislev as, according to tradition, the evening is considered part of the following day and therefore all Jewish holidays begin on the evening before the day of the holiday. The first candle is put in the Menorah from the person's right, and an additional candle is added each night. However, the candles are lit from left to right to stress the importance of each day of Chanukah. A special additional candle is lit each night. This candle is called the Shamash, or server; it is lit first, and then used to kindle the other candles.

2. We eat LATKES, or pancakes, which are made with oil or other fats to symbolize the cruse of oil found in the Temple by Judah the Maccabee.

3. Children usually receive CHANUKAH GELT (money). They play with DREIDLACH (square tops), which have the following Hebrew letters on their sides: N-G-H-SH, an abbreviation of the Hebrew words "Nes Gadol Hayah Sham," which means "A great miracle happened there."

4. Plays about Hannah and her seven sons, Eliezer the Priest, Judah the Maccabee, etc. are presented by children to teach them how to be brave and good Jews.

5. Hallel (Psalms of praise) is chanted to thank God for His help to the Maccabees.

TRANSLATION OF BLESSINGS FOR CHANUKAH

FOR LIGHTING CHANUKAH CANDLES

Blessed are You, Lord our God, King of the Universe, who sanctified us with His commandments and commanded us to kindle the light of Chanukah.

Blessed are You, Lord our God, King of the Universe, who performed miracles for our ancestors in those days at this season.

Blessed are You, Lord our God, King of the Universe, who kept us alive and preserved us and enabled us to reach this season.

FOR EATING LATKES

Blessed are You, Lord our God, King of the Universe, creator of all kinds of foods.

CHANUKAH STORIES

Judith and Holofernes

In the city of Bethulia, there lived a pious Jewish woman whose husband was killed in the battle with the Greeks. Her name was Judith. One day, a Syrian general, Holofernes, besieged her city and was ready to destroy it and kill all its inhabitants. Judith asked permission from the Elders of the city to try to save the people and, at the same time, to avenge her husband's death.

In the evening, she took some wine and cheese with her, stole out of the city, and appeared before Holofernes. She offered to help him conquer the city. Holofernes, not suspecting anything, and thinking that Judith was willing to be a spy, agreed to this. She then offered him some of her strong wine, as well as some of her tasty cheese. Holofernes drank the wine and ate the cheese with gusto. This made him very drowsy, and soon he fell asleep. Then Judith cut off his head with his own sword, tucked it under her arm, and entered the city. In the morning, the Syrians saw their commander's head on the top of a pole at the gates of the city. They became very frightened, and the people of Bethulia attacked the confused Syrians and defeated them.

To honor the brave Judith, it has become a custom among Jews to eat dairy dishes on Chanukah to remind them of the cheese which Judith fed Holofernes.

(Jewish Folklore)

Latkes

A poor man once came home and told his wife that he had been to a rich man's home and had seen him eating latkes. "Oh, if I could only have some latkes," he said. "After all, it is Chanukah!" His wife answered, "I would like to make some latkes for you, but I have no cream."

"Well, make them without cream."

"But I have no butter or oil."

"Make them without butter or oil."

"But I have no sugar."

"Make them without sugar."

His wife conceded defeat, and made the latkes without any sugar, oil or cream—she made them just from raw potatoes. When the poor man tasted the raw potatoes, he spat the mixture out, and said, "I can't understand the rich people. How can they possibly like and enjoy food like this!"

Washington and the Chanukah Candle

The winter of 1777 in Valley Forge was a bitter one. We were all sitting and waiting, for what? No one knew. I was the only Jewish soldier in Valley Forge at that time. We were hungry and cold, and some were without shoes. Many soldiers cursed George Washington, but I believed that he was right. On a number of occasions, I had seen him walk at night among the rows of sleeping soldiers, look at them with pity, and sometimes bend and cover some of them, like a father covering his children.

I recall my father in Poland being forced to dress in a bear's skin and dance before drunken Polish nobles for their amusement. What an insult and shame to my noble father. As soon as an opportunity presented itself, I ran away to America, and joined Washington's forces. I prayed every day that Washington should be victorious.

Before I left my father's home, my father gave me a silver Menorah, and said:

"My son, do not forget to light the candles of Chanukah wherever you will be. They will light your way to freedom."

I always kept my promise to my father. When Chanukah came, while I was in Valley Forge, I took out my Menorah, lit the first candle, and chanted the blessing. The Menorah suddenly reminded me of my suffering parents, brothers and sisters, and my decision to fight for freedom under Washington became stronger. I sat before the Menorah and cried, as I remembered my father's house.

Suddenly I felt a soft hand touch my shoulder. As I turned around, I saw General Washington looking at me with inquisitive eyes.

"Why are you crying, soldier?" he asked. "Is it because of the bitter cold?" I suddenly forgot that I, a private, faced the commander-in-chief, and began to talk to him like a son to a father.

"I am crying and praying for your victory, General, and I am sure that we will win because we are fighting for a just cause. We want to bring freedom to ourselves and others."

The general shook my hand and thanked me. He then sat beside me and asked, "What is this lamp?" I told him about the significance of the Menorah, and that the little candle symbolizes the fight of the Maccabees for freedom.

Washington then said, 'You are a Jew, a son of the prophets, and if you predict we will win, we shall win." He shook my hand and disappeared in the enveloping darkness.

George Washington won. He later became the first president of the United States. The bitter nights of Valley Forge were forgotten. The only thing which I remembered was my meeting with George Washington.

However, I was sure that Washington had forgotten about the Chanukah incident a long time ago. I moved to New York City. One Chanukah night I lit my Menorah and put it on the window sill as custom demands. Suddenly a knock was heard on the door. I opened it and was astonished to see General Washington standing there. The President of the United States himself was standing in my doorway. What an honor! As he entered, he said to me, "I passed the street and saw the Menorah which resembled the Menorah in Valley Forge. That little candle and your words brought light into my heart on that fateful night, and I never forgot it. Soon you will be honored, together with the other Valley Forge heroes, by the Government of the United States."

That night the General received the Menorah from me as a gift. I was too excited to say anything as the President shook my hand, thanked me and departed with my father's Menorah.

CHANUKAH QUESTIONS

True or False

Mattathias was a young general.

Judah the Maccabee was the son of Mattathias.

Antiochus was a Greek king.

We eat Homantashen on Chanukah.

We light eight candles on Chanukah because of a small jar of oil.

Latkes are eaten on Chanukah because Sarah, the wife of Abraham made them for the visiting angels.

Judah lit the Menorah in the Second Temple.

We light eight candles on the first night of Chanukah.

Latkes are eaten because Jewish women made them so hard that their husbands used them as ammunition against the Greeks.

A Dreidel is a square top.

Judah was called the "Maccabee" because he was the keeper of the bees.

Hannah's children were killed because they did not bow to an idol.

Why

Why do we light candles for eight days on Chanukah?

Why was Judah called the "Maccabee"?

Why do we play with Dreidlach on Chanukah?

Why do we eat Latkes on Chanukah?

Why was Eliezer killed by the Greeks?

Draw a Line Under the Correct Answer

Kohen Gadol means: high priest, general, big man.

Maccabee means: Hammer, player, fighter.

We celebrate Chanukah in the month of Tishri, Elul, Kislev.

Menorah is an organization, lamp, city.

The Temple was in Jerusalem, Haifa, Tel Aviv.

General Questions

Is Chanukah observed because we are commanded to do so in the
Torah?

Could you show the similarity between the Maccabean fight for
independence and the fight of Israel for independence in 1948?

Why do you like Chanukah?

How do you observe Chanukah?

Why is it important for every Jewish boy and girl to celebrate
Chanukah?

Do you remember the blessings over Chanukah candles?

Do you know what the four letters inscribed on the Dreidel mean?

What does the word Chanukah mean?

Tu Bishevat

ARBOR DAY

The Jewish Arbor Day is called Tu Bishevat. It is celebrated on the 15th day of the Hebrew month of Shevat (January or February). "Tu" in Hebrew equals "15" (Letter T=9, Letter U=6). On this day the winter season ends in Israel. The heavy rains come down no more, and the sap begins to stir in the trees. Though it is mid-winter in America, in Israel Spring is beginning.

Tu Bishevat is also called Rosh Hashanah Lailonot, The New Year for Trees. Tradition tells us that on this day, God decides which plants shall survive and which shall die during the coming year. This teaches us that trees and plants are living organisms, and we should take good care of them.

Tu Bishevat is sometimes called Chag Hanetiot (Holiday of Planting Trees). Young and old Jews in Israel go out to the hills and valleys on this day and plant tens of thousands of young saplings. They replant forests, and seek to change the desert and rocky hills into habitable, life-giving areas.

On this day, the Jews throughout the world collect and contribute money, and thus do their share in planting trees in Israel. A people who for centuries were foced to live in dark, drab ghettos where almost nothing grew, always found joy in Tu Bishevat. They find even more happiness in this holiday today, when the Holy Land is again becoming "a land flowing with milk and honey."

SPECIAL CUSTOMS OF TU BISHEVAT

Since Tu Bishevat is an agricultural holiday, it is customary to eat on this day those fruits which grow in Israel. We eat Boksor (carob tree fruit), figs, dates, almonds and raisins.

The Sephardim in Jerusalem spend the entire night of the 15th of Shevat in their synagogue. They read portions of the Torah and Talmud referring to agriculture in Israel, and the fruits that grow there.

The Chassidim pray on Tu Bishevat that the ethrogim (citrons) should grow beautiful and perfect for the Sukkoth holiday.

BLESSINGS FOR TU BISHEVAT

FOR ALL FRUITS

Blessed are You, our Lord, King of the Universe, creator of the fruit of the tree.

TU BISHEVAT FOLKLORE

Honi Ha' Maagel

Honi Ha' Maagel was a saintly man. Once when there was a drought in the land of Israel, the people came and begged him to pray for rain. No sooner had Honi finished his prayer than rain came down in torrents. The people begged him to slow down the rain. Honi prayed again, and the rain began to fall in a natural manner.

One day Honi happened to walk alongside a farm and he saw an old man planting a carob tree near his house.

"How long does it take for the carob tree to bear fruit?" asked Honi. The old man answered, "It takes 70 years to grow and begin bearing fruit."

"Then why do you plant this tree? Do you expect to enjoy its fruit? You are an old man now," said Honi.

"I enjoyed carobs from trees which my parents and grandparents planted, and I want my grandchildren to enjoy the fruit when I am gone," answered the old man.

Honi walked along. He felt tired and sat down to rest. He fell asleep, and miraculously kept on sleeping for 70 years. Grass grew around him and over him, protecting him from the sun and rain.

After 70 years, Honi awoke from his long sleep. He noticed a man picking carobs from the tree which he had seen being planted. Honi asked him, "Where is the man who planted this tree?"

"Oh, that was my grandfather," answered the man.

"So I was sleeping for some time," Honi thought.

Honi went to his home and inquired about his little son and wife. His wife was dead, and so was his son, but his grandson was alive.

"I am Honi Ha' Maagel," he said, but no one believed him. He went to the Yeshivah where he used to teach, and found sages discussing a certain point of law. One of them said, "In the days of Honi Ha' Maagel we could find an easy solution to every difficult question simply by asking him, but now we have difficulty in solving many points of law."

"I am Honi," said the old man, but no one believed him. Some even scolded him for showing disrespect for the memory of a great sage. Honi went back to the place where he had slept, prayed to God, and died peacefully in his sleep.

Some days later, his great-grandchildren, while playing in that spot, found the body of a very old man. They did not know that it was their great-grandfather, the great sage Honi Ha' Maagel.

The King and the Figs

Once a king passed through a village. He asked an old man who was planting a fig tree, "How old are you, my man?"

"One hundred years," answered the old man.

"And you expect to eat figs from this tree?" asked the king. Answered the old man, "Your majesty, if I live long enough, I may be able to eat the fruits of this tree. If not, I will at least leave figs for my descendants, as my parents have done before."

The king was pleased with his answer. After a number of years, the king happened to pass the same village again and found the old man still alive. The old man filled a basket with figs from the tree which he had planted, and presented it to the king. The king was pleased with the gift; he filled the same basket with gold coins, and presented it to the old man.

A jealous neighbor of the old man happened to find out about this. So he filled a big basket with figs and presented it to the king, thinking that the king would also fill his basket with gold. However, the king became angry and ordered his guards to throw the fruit in the neighbor's face. Heartbroken, the man came home and told his wife what had happened, and how the king had treated him differently than he had treated the old man.

His wife comforted him by saying, "You are lucky that they were soft figs and not hard lemons."

TU BISHEVAT QUESTIONS

True or False

Tu Bishevat means 20 days in the month of Shevat.
Tu Bishevat is the Jewish Arbor day.
On Tu Bishevat we eat Israeli fruit.
Tu Bishevat is called Rosh Hashanah for trees.
We plant trees in Israel on Tu Bishevat.

When

When do we observe Tu Bishevat?
When did the Jews first settle in Israel?

General Questions

What is the meaning of the letters Teth and Vav?
Why is it important to have the land of Israel full of trees?
Why is it important to celebrate Tu Bishevat?
Do you recall the expression used often in the Torah to describe the land of Israel?
Do you know the names of some cities in Israel?
Did you ever visit Israel?
Did some of your relatives ever visit Israel?
Did you ever plant some trees in Israel by contributing to the Jewish National Fund?
Did you ever count how many trees are near your home?

Purim

The festival of Purim is celebrated on the 14th day of the
Hebrew month of Adar (February). In a Hebrew leap year,
when there are two Hebrew months of Adar, it comes on the
14th day of Adar II.

The name Purim comes from the word "Pur" meaning "lot."
Haman cast lots to decide which month and day would be best
to exterminate the Jews of Persia. Haman's plot did not succeed.
The Jews were saved on this day, and therefore we celebrate it
as a holiday.

The Story of Purim

During the period 450—350 B.C.E., there was a ruler in Persia
by the name of Ahasuerus, who ruled over 120 provinces and
lands in which most of the Jews of that time lived. In those days,

the King, a ruler of one of the most powerful kingdoms, often spent time in making merry at drinking parties with his friends. Once he decided that his Queen, Vashti, should come and dance before his friends, though it was not usual for a queen to dance before strangers. When Vashti refused, the King became very angry and decided to get rid of her, for fear the women of the land would follow Vashti's example.

Ahasuerus then chose a new queen by means of a beauty contest. Her name was Hadassah, or Esther, a cousin of Mordecai, a Jewish leader. Upon Mordecai's advice, Esther did not tell the King that she was Jewish.

After Vashti's dismissal, Haman the Amalekite was appointed Prime Minister, and everybody was ordered to bow down to him. He disliked the Jews, and especially their leader, Mordecai, because he refused to bow down to him. So Haman, his wife Zeresh, and his friends plotted to do away with all the Jews.

At a time when the King was very drunk, Haman persuaded Ahasuerus to sign a decree giving Haman permission to kill all Jews in the kingdom. Haman described these Jews as traitors, but in reality, they were the King's most loyal friends. The date for the massacre, the 13th of Adar, was chosen by Haman and his friends by drawing lots (which in Persian were called Purim).

Later, Mordecai by chance overheard two of Haman's friends discussing ways and means of poisoning the King. Mordecai hurried to inform his friend Harvonah, one of the King's officers, about the plot. Both plotters were caught in action and executed. Mordecai's noble deed was written down in the Book of Chronicles of the Persian Kings.

One night King Ahasuerus could not fall asleep. In order to amuse himself, he ordered that the Book of the Kings be brought, and that portions be read to him. It happened that the page opened first by the reader related the good deed of Mordecai. "Did this man, Mordecai, receive his reward?" asked the King.

The answer was, "No". Desiring to reward Mordecai, the King decided to ask his friend Haman for suggestions.

Hastily, Haman was brought to the King. The King asked him, "How should I reward the man whom I like best?" "Whom does the King like best if not me?" thought Haman. He said, "I would suggest that this man should be dressed in the King's clothes, be put on the King's favorite horse, and be led through the streets of Shushan, and a great lord should proclaim that this is the man whom the King likes best." "In that case, my friend," said the King, "go into the next room and you shall find the man who will receive this honor." Haman was very disappointed and astonished when he saw that the man was Mordecai, his enemy. Nevertheless, Haman had to obey the King's order.

While leading Mordecai through the streets of Shushan and proclaiming him the King's favorite, Haman passed his own house. Zeresh, Haman's wife, seeing the procession, was sure that her husband was being honored. Who else in the kingdom could be so honored besides the King himself? She thought that the one leading the horse resembled Mordecai, the enemy of her husband. She therefore spilled a pail of dirty water on the one who led the horse. She nearly fell out the window when she realized that Mordecai was the man being honored, not Haman.

After this incident, Haman made all preparations to get rid of the Jews, especially Mordecai, his worst enemy, on the 13th of Adar. After all, he had a document signed by the King himself. When Mordecai was informed about Haman's plot, realizing that time was running short, he decided to act fast. He sent secret directions to Esther to act quickly, to see the King and upset Haman's plan. Esther sent word to Mordecai to tell all the Jews to fast for three days and pray to God, and she would do so also, before she went to inform and persuade the King.

Esther invited the King and Haman to a private party. Haman was happy with this invitation. But his surprise was great when, at the party, Esther disclosed to the King not only that she was

Jewish, but that on the 13th of Adar, she might be killed. When the King heard this, he immediately commanded that Haman, his ten sons, and his henchmen should be hung on a gallows 50 cubits high, which Haman had erected in order to hang Mordecai. He also ordered that all Hamanites be killed on the same day that Haman planned to kill all the Jews.

Upon the suggestion of Esther, Ahasuerus appointed Mordecai, who once saved his life, to the post of Prime Minister in place of Haman. Esther and Mordecai then sent letters to all communities of Jews to observe the holiday of Purim on the 14th of Adar; and, to this day, it is still celebrated.

Ahasuerus the King, Esther the Queen, and Mordecai the Prime Minister, lived happily ever after.

SPECIAL CUSTOMS OBSERVED ON PURIM

1. The Megillah (scroll) of Esther, or Story of Purim, is read on the 14th day of Adar.

2. During the reading of the Megillah, the children make noise with gragers (noise-makers) whenever the name of Haman is mentioned. This is a way of booing Haman.

3. Three-cornered poppy-seed pastries called Hamantashen are eaten to symbolize the hat of Haman. Hamantashen also represent the feast that Esther prepared at which time three people, Ahasuerus, Esther, and Haman were present, and the fates of Mordecai, the Jews, and Haman were decided.

4. A special Purim feast (Purim Seudah) takes place in the late afternoon of Purim, and is one of the happiest of Jewish traditional customs.

5. Gifts are given to the poor (Matanoth Laevyonim) and gifts are exchanged between members of families and their friends (Shalach Manoth).

6. A fast (Fast of Esther) is held on the 13th day of Adar, the day that Haman was to carry out his plan to kill all the Jews.

7. Purim itself is celebrated on the next day, the 14th of Adar, when the Jews defeated Haman and his friends. During a leap year, Purim is celebrated on the 14th of Adar II.

8. The day after Purim is called Shushan Purim. It is celebrated as a semi-holiday in accordance with the custom of the Jews who lived in the Persian capitol of Shushan, and who celebrated Purim a day later, on the 15th of Adar.

9. Ad-Lo-Yodah is a Hebrew phrase used during Purim. It implies a happy and carefree celebration to the point where one is doubtful as to his sober condition. Literally, Ad means "till"—Lo means "did not"—Yodah means "know." According to tradition, the Jews were to drink and make merry on Purim. In Israel, a huge celebration called Ad-Lo-Yodah is staged, with floats and banners depicting the Purim characters and story.

TRANSLATION OF BLESSINGS FOR PURIM

BEFORE THE MEGILLAH

Blessed are You, Lord our God, King of the Universe, who sanctified us with His commandments and commanded us to read the Megillah.

Blessed are You, Lord our God, King of the Universe, who performed miracles for our fathers in those days and at this season.

Blessed are You, Lord our God, King of the Universe, who kept us alive and helped us reach this season.

FOR EATING A HAMANTASH

Blessed are You, Lord our God, King of the Universe, creator of all kinds of food.

PURIM FOLKLORE

The Magic Drink

Once, on the eve of Purim, Simcha the tailor was brought into court under the complaint that he had gotten drunk and created a disturbance in town by breaking windows in his neighbor's store.

The judge, who was well disposed, felt that a Jew had the right to start celebrating Purim ahead of time. However, for the sake of the record, he asked Simcha for a "valid" reason why he should not be detained.

Simcha answered, "I felt depressed on the eve of Purim, because my wife did not have enough money to bake hamantashen. To cheer myself up, I took one drink. Now according to our sages, a Jew who takes a drink becomes a new man. To celebrate my becoming a new man, I had to take a drink. Then, I and the other man had to get acquainted, so we each took a drink. Naturally, after getting acquainted, we had to celebrate our new-found friendship, and," Simcha concluded, "this is why I am here in court." The judge dismissed the case.

The Barber of Karzum

There was once a man by the name of Haman who was a barber for 25 years in the Persian town of Karzum. Haman was an ambitious man, and when he saw, after working for 25 years, that he remained poor, he decided to join the Persian army and seek adventure in distant countries.

Soon a war broke out and the Persians suffered defeat. The Persians fled into the wilderness where they felt safe from the victorious enemy. However, they suffered hunger and thirst, and many died. Haman, one of the fleeing soldiers, went around begging some food from the other men. No one gave him anything until he approached a Jewish soldier by the name of Mordecai, who gave him some water and a piece of bread. Haman felt so thankful to the Jew that he offered to become Mordecai's slave. He signed a bill of sale on a parchment, and gave it to Mordecai.

Finally, the remnants of the Persian army made their way home. Haman moved to Shushan and became a barber. Mordecai settled among his fellow Jews, and because of his wisdom and piety, he became their leader.

One day Haman, wandering in a field, found a treasure hidden behind a rock. He bought a beautiful palace in Shushan, and in a short time became known as the richest man in the city. He became a frequent guest in the palace of King Ahasuerus. The King liked Haman for his smooth tongue, and finally appointed him Prime Minister. Haman then decreed that all Persians must bow to him whenever he passed by.

One day, Haman spotted Mordecai in the crowd. Everyone bowed to Haman. Only Mordecai stood erect. Haman became frightened: What if Mordecai presented to the King the parchment which Haman had signed, claiming Haman as his slave? His days as Prime Minister of Persia would be few.

Haman decided to get rid of Mordecai, before Mordecai got him. He came before King Ahasuerus, and told him, "There is a nation among your vassal nations, which is different from all of us. It has strange customs and acts very suspiciously, praying to an invisible God. For the protection of your empire, we should get rid of them."

Ahasuerus, not a very clever man, and a lazy person who did not like to bother with details, left it to his clever Prime Minister to settle the question. Haman, right then and there, asked the King to sign a parchment, prepared in advance, which would give him the power to kill all Jews, including Mordecai, their leader.

And so the struggle between Mordecai the Jew and Haman the Amalekite began, and resulted finally in Haman's defeat.

Mordecai and the Three Students

When Mordecai learned about the decree, signed by the King, to kill all Jews, he became very upset. He walked through the streets of Shushan trying to decide how to help his fellow Jews. On the way, three little Jewish boys were walking calmly home from school. Their calmness impressed him, and he asked the first boy, "What did you learn in school today that makes you so calm?"

The boy answered, "I learned, 'Be not afraid of sudden terror, nor of the wickedness of the wicked, when it comes.'"

He asked the second boy, "What did you learn today in school?"

"I learned," answered the second child, "the sentence which reads, 'Take counsel, and it shall be brought to nothing; speak the word and it will not stand; for God is with us.'"

"What did you learn, my boy?" asked Mordecai of the third boy. "I learned the sentence, 'I am your Lord who will help you as I have done in the past, and I will carry you and will save you (in the future).'"

As soon as Mordecai heard this, his mood changed and he became happy. He felt that God had sent him a message through the mouths of the three little boys, and he was sure that God would save the Jews and punish Haman.

PURIM QUESTIONS

Draw a Line Under the Correct Answer

Esther's other name was Rachel, Hadassah, Miriam.

Mordecai was Esther's father, uncle, cousin.

Ahasuerus was the king, the prime minister, the butler.

The Megillah is a book, a scroll, a place in Israel.

Haman was a hay salesman, a prime minister, a scientist.

Vashti was a queen, a washwoman, a dancer.

How and If

How did you observe Purim last year?

If a girl, did you take part in a Queen Esther contest?

If a boy, did you ever take part in a Hamantashen contest?

What part did you ever play in a Purim play?

Did you ever take part in an Ad Lo Yodah celebration? Did you
  ever see one?

True or False

Esther was chosen beauty queen in Atlantic City.

Vashti lived in Persia.

Mordecai rode on the king's horse.

Esther was the wife of Ahasuerus.

Shushan was the capitol of Persia.

The Megillah is the story of Purim.

Purim is celebrated in the month of Nissan.

We eat Hamantashen on Purim because Moses gave the Jews
  Hamantashen when they left Egypt.

Why

Why was Vashti dismissed as queen?

Why did Haman want to kill the Jews?

Why did the King command Haman to let Mordecai ride on his
favorite horse?

Why do we celebrate Purim on the 14th of Adar?

Why do Hamantashen have three corners?

Why was Mordecai rewarded by the king?

Why was Haman hanged?

General Questions

Why is the holiday called Purim?

When is Purim celebrated if it occurs in a leap year?

When is Shushan Purim celebrated?

When is the Fast of Esther observed?

Why do you like Purim?

Why is it important to celebrate Purim?

Can you remember other historical events similar to the Purim
story?

How did you celebrate Purim last year?

How many Purim songs do you know?

Pesach

PASSOVER

The holiday of Pesach is celebrated for eight days from the eve of the 15th to nightfall of the 23rd of the Hebrew Month of Nissan (March or April). The first two and the last two days are full holidays, when no work is done. The middle four days are called "Chol-Hamoed" or semi-holiday, during which time work is permitted.

The holiday is known by the following names:

CHAG HAPESACH   The Holiday of Passover, because when the last plague was brought on the Egyptians, Jewish homes were passed over and not visited by the plague.

CHAG HAMATZOTH   The Holiday of Matzoth, because during

this holiday we are permitted to eat only Matzoth (unleavened bread).

Z'MAN CHERUSENU   The Season of Our Freedom, because at this time the Jews were freed from slavery in Egypt.

CHAG HEAVIV   The Holiday of Spring, which is the time of the year when the holiday is celebrated.

ECHAD M'SHALOSH REGALIM   One of the three Walking Holidays. The three Walking Holidays were Pesach, Shavuoth and Sukkoth.

On each of the three Walking Holidays, each male Jew was commanded by the Torah to make a pilgrimage up to the Temple in Jerusalem. On each of the pilgrimages, a gift was brought. On Pesach—the Omer (first ripe barley). On Shavuoth—the Bikkurim (first ripe wheat); and on Sukkoth—the four kinds of fruit, and special sacrifices.

The Story of Passover

Passover is one of the most ancient Jewish holidays and is considered the Jewish independence holiday, since it marks the exodus of the Jews from Egypt about 1300 B.C.E., after being enslaved there for 210 years.

Our ancestor, Jacob, and his sons and their families, settled in the province of Goshen in Egypt, at the invitation of Jacob's son Joseph, who had become second in power to Pharaoh, the King of Egypt. However, after Joseph died and a new king had come to power, the Jews were enslaved, and harsh laws were passed in order to destroy them. The new king ordered the Jews to make mortar and bricks and to build treasure cities. He also ordered that every Jewish-born boy be drowned. However, the more he oppressed the Jews, the stronger they became and the more they multiplied.

During this period when the Jews were slaves, a Jewish boy was born to Amram and Yocheved, the Levites. They hid the boy for three months, so that Pharaoh's men should not find him. They could not hide him, however, any longer. So his mother Yocheved put the boy in a basket, and placed the basket in the tall reeds on the banks of the Nile River. It happened that Princess Bathia, daughter of the King, came upon the basket and found the boy. She adopted him and called him Moses, because she had taken him out of the water. Moses grew up in the palace of the princess.

One day Moses saw an Egyptian overseer beating a Jew mercilessly. He killed the Egyptian and saved the Jew, but he then was forced to flee from Egypt. He settled in the land of Midian as a shepherd, and he married a shepherdess, Zipporah, the youngest daughter of the priest, Jethro.

When Moses was tending his sheep one day, he saw a strange sight: a small bush was burning but was not being destroyed by the fire. When he came close to investigate, the voice of God spoke to him from the bush and ordered him to return to Egypt and save the Jews from slavery. Moses followed God's command and on his way back to Egypt, he met his older brother, Aaron, who accompanied him to Egypt. They both came to Pharaoh, and in the name of God demanded that he let the Jews go out of Egypt. Pharaoh answered their demand by increasing the hardships of the Jews. In return, God then brought ten plagues upon Egypt. They were as follows:

1. Blood (all water turned into blood)
2. Frogs
3. Lice
4. Wild beasts
5. Cattle disease
6. Skin disease
7. Hail
8. Locusts
9. Darkness
10. Killing of Egyptian first-born

When the tenth plague hit Egypt, the Angel of Death killed the first-born Egyptians, but passed over the homes of the Jews. Pharaoh, whose first-born son was killed and who, as a first-born, was in danger himself, called Moses and Aaron and ordered them to take the Jews out of Egypt. The Jews left Egypt as free people, and moved to the desert on their way to the promised land of Canaan. The exodus occurred on the 15th day of Nissan, in the spring of the year. In their haste to leave Egypt, the Jews took the dough with them before it had risen and become leavened. They baked the dough into flat cakes (matzoth) in the hot desert sun.

So the Jews were finally freed from slavery. However, as long as they had not crossed the Red Sea, there was always the danger that Pharaoh might pursue them and try to bring them back to Egypt. And this is just what happened. After the plagues were gone, Pharaoh changed his mind, and his army pursued the Jews. The Jews found themselves between the waters of the Red Sea and the army of Pharaoh. God then told Moses to stretch out his hand toward the Red Sea. Moses followed God's command, and the waters of the sea split in two, clearing the way for the Jews to pass on dry land. When Pharaoh's army followed in their path, the waters returned to their usual position, and the Egyptians were drowned. The Jews were at last completely free. They sang a song of praise and thanks to the Lord.

CUSTOMS AND PRACTICES OF PASSOVER

1. "Maoth Chitim" (literally, money for wheat) is given before Passover to the less fortunate members of the community, to enable every Jew to celebrate the Holiday of Freedom properly along with the rest of his people.

2. Since during Passover the Jew is not permitted to possess any Chometz (any food containing in whole or in part any of the five species of fermented grain, and/or dishes, containers and other implements associated with such food), he is required to effect a sale to a non-Jew of all his Chometz. This is done through an

agent, usually the Rabbi of the community, and is called "Mechirath Chometz," or the selling of the Chometz.

3. The ceremony of "Bedikath Chometz" (searching for Chometz) is observed the night before Passover. Pieces of bread are placed on the window sills. Then, by the light of a candle, the bread is brushed into a container with a feather. The feather and the candle are put into a bag together with the container; the following morning, the bag is burned ("Biur Chometz": burning of the Chometz).

4. Matzoth (thin cakes of flour containing no salt or yeast) are eaten during the eight days of Passover instead of bread. This commemorates the flight of the Israelites from Egypt. In their hurried escape, they took with them unleavened dough as part of their food supply.

5. On the first two nights of Passover, the Hagadah (from the Hebrew "L'Hagid", meaning "to tell") is read, recounting the story of Passover. The first two nights are called the Seder Nights (the Hebrew word "Seder" means "order"). Passover is celebrated according to tradition, and in the order prescribed by the sages. This order of procedure is indicated in the Hagadah. It is customary to recline during the Seder ceremony, which is conducted at a table set in a prescribed order. The first part of the Hagadah is read before the evening meal. Then there is an intermission for a holiday feast. After the meal, the Hagadah reading is completed.

6. Three Matzoth are placed on the Seder plate in honor of Kohanim, Levites and Israelites who did not forget their language, customs and traditions while in Egypt. The unity of all Jews made the exodus from Egypt possible.

There is another reason why three Matzoth are placed on the Seder plate. Ordinarily, on every holiday and Sabbath, two loaves of bread or Challoth, are placed on the table. These two loaves, called the "Lechem Mishneh" (double bread) are necessary to make the proper blessing. During Passover, however, Matzoth are used. Since according to tradition, we are required to eat from the "Poor Bread" on Passover, the middle Matzah is used for this purpose. It is broken in two; part of it becomes the Afikomen, which is concealed temporarily, and the remaining piece serves as the "Poor Bread."

7. "Maror" (bitter herb) is eaten as a symbol of the suffering of our ancestors in Egypt. Long leaf celery can be used for Maror in place of horse-radish. In fact, it is better than horse-radish, since celery is sweet first, then becomes bitter as it grows older. Celery can thus serve as a reminder of the sweet and bitter times that the Jews spent in Egypt. When the Jews came to Egypt in the days of Joseph, life was sweet for them, but later after Joseph's death, life in Egypt became very bitter.

8. "Charoseth" (a mixture of wine, apples and nuts) is eaten to recall the mortar which our ancestors used for erecting buildings in Egypt while slaves of Pharoah.

9. An egg and roasted meat are used to symbolize the Pascal sacrifices brought to the Temple by our ancestors when the Jews lived in Israel. The egg was chosen to represent the holiday sacrifice because of its special qualities. All other foods are softened by long cooking, but an egg becomes hard. So, too, with the Jews: the longer they suffered in Egypt, the stronger they became. An egg is also round, symbolizing the cycle of life and death, freedom and oppression.

10. Salt water is used as a symbol of the tears shed by our ancestors while in Egypt. The salt water also may symbolize the Red Sea which was crossed by the Jews after leaving Egypt.

11. "Karpas" (vegetable) is eaten to symbolize the growth of vegetation in the spring.

12. "Kneidlach" (Matzoth balls) are eaten either in soup or with meat dishes during the Passover meal. Kneidlach, or Matzah balls, are usually eaten on the Seder night as a symbol of the rocks which fell upon the enemy when Joshua fought the Canaanites. This event happened on the eve of Passover.

13. Parsley is dipped into salt water to symbolize the miracle of the Red Sea which separated. White Maror is dipped into the Charoseth to symbolize the bitterness of life for the Jews in Egypt.

14. A sandwich of Matzoth and Maror is eaten on the Seder night. This custom was introduced by the sage, Hillel.

15. The youngest member of the family asks the "Fier Kashes" (the four questions), requesting an explanation of the special acts that are performed on Passover, at the Seder table. In reply, the father reads from the Hagadah the story of Jewish suffering in Egypt, and the exodus from that country. The reasons Matzoth, Maror, and other things are eaten are also indicated in the Hagadah.

16. The story of the ten plagues is related. God plagued the Egyptians in order to compel them to free the Jews from slavery. When reciting the ten plagues, wine is spilled from our cups for each plague. This denotes that our happiness is not complete, knowing that human beings have been killed, despite the fact that they were our enemies. According to our Sages, we should not rejoice when our enemy is beaten.

17. Four cups of wine are drunk, symbolizing the four promises which God made to the Jews in Egypt. They were (a) "I Shall Bring You Out"; (b) "I Shall Save You"; (c) "I Shall Redeem You"; and (d) "I Shall Take You."

18. Placed on the Seder table is an extra cup of wine, often referred to as the fifth cup, from which no one drinks. This is in honor of the Prophet Elijah. The door is open to admit Elijah who, it is traditionally held, visits every Jewish home on Passover and blesses the people. Elijah was the most beloved prophet among Jews, and many legends and folk stories have been told about him. The fifth cup also symbolizes the fifth promise of God, "And I Shall Bring You into the Land."

19. The Seder meal is completed with the eating of the Afikomen (from the Greek word meaning "dessert"), consisting of the broken piece of Matzah which the master of the house concealed

at the beginning of the Seder service. It symbolizes the Pascal sacrifice which was eaten in the Temple at the end of the meal. It has become a practice for the youngest child to obtain the Afikomen and demand a ransom for its return, for we cannot end the Seder service without it. Children play an active part in the Passover celebration. God commands us to tell the children about the Exodus, so that they may learn to cherish freedom and be proud of their heritage and traditions.

20. At the end of the Seder service, songs are sung, the last of which is "Chad Gadyah" ("One Only Kid"). This is a simple song, the moral of which is that God is the Supreme Judge of the universe.

21. The Song of Songs, written by King Solomon, is chanted on the morning of Passover in the synagogue. It describes nature coming to life in the spring, when Passover is celebrated.

22. On the second day of Passover, the counting of the "Omer" is begun. (Omer was an ancient measure of grain). When the Temple stood in Jerusalem, the Jewish farmer would bring an Omer of the first ripe grain to the Temple to express his thanks to God. The Torah commands us to count 49 days from the bringing of the Omer on Passover, and on the 50th day to celebrate Shavuoth.

TRANSLATION OF BLESSINGS FOR PASSOVER

FOR LIGHTING CANDLES

Blessed are You, Lord our God, King of the Universe, who has sanctified us by His commandments and has commanded us to light the festival candle.

Blessed are You, Lord our God, King of the Universe, who has kept us alive and preserved us and enabled us to reach this season.

FOR TALITH

Blessed are You, Lord our God, King of the Universe, who has sanctified us by His commandments and has commanded us to wrap ourselves in the fringed garment.

MORNING KIDDUSH AND BLESSING ON WINE

And Moses declared the feasts of God to the children of Israel. Blessed are You, Lord our God, King of the Universe, who created the fruit of the vine.

FOR MATZAH

Blessed are You, Lord our God, King of the Universe, who brings forth bread from the earth.

Blessed are You, Lord our God, King of the Universe, who has sanctified us by His commandments and commanded us to eat Matzah.

FOR BITTER HERBS

Blessed are You, Lord our God, King of the Universe, who has sanctified us by His commandments and commanded us to eat bitter herbs.

FOR VEGETABLES

Blessed are You, Lord our God, King of the Universe, Creator of the fruit of the earth.

FOR FRUIT

Blessed are You, Lord our God, King of the Universe, Creator of the fruit of the tree.

PESACH FOLKLORE

Moses the Shepherd

One day while Moses was tending his flock in the land of Midian, he noticed that a little lamb was running away. He chased after it, but the lamb ran faster until it came to a spring and began to drink water from it. Moses said, "My dear little lamb, if I had known that you were thirsty, I would not have chased after you." Moses tenderly cradled the lamb in his arms and carried it back to the flock. When God saw this, God said, "Moses is the right man to be the leader of the Jews and take them out of Egypt, as he is a man full of pity." And so, as Moses was walking back to his flock carrying the tired little lamb, God appeared to him in the burning bush and commanded him to go back to Egypt and lead the Jews out of that country.

A Bad Dream

Pharaoh had three advisers, Jethro, Job and Balaam. One night Pharaoh dreamed that an old man, a giant, appeared. He took all the elders, magicians, and great men of Egypt, and put them on one side of a pair of scales, and on the other he put a kid (baby goat), and the kid outweighed all those Egyptians.

In the morning, the king called in his advisers, told them his dream, and asked them to interpret it. Balaam answered: "Your Majesty, the dream means that a child will be born among the Hebrews, and he will destroy all the Egyptians. Danger threatens all Egypt."

"What shall I do?" asked the king.

Jethro talked first. He advised the king to lighten the burden of the Hebrews because the God of Israel avenges all who oppress them. Job remained silent. Balaam, who hated the Jews very

much, advised the king to destroy the Jews. He advised the king
to throw all the new-born sons of Israel into the Nile river, until
no men would remain among them.

Jethro, who spoke up for the Jews, was honored by becoming
the father-in-law of Moses. Job, who kept quiet, was punished
by God with pestilence and poverty for some time. Balaam, who
opposed the Jews, was killed by Moses in the battle between the
king of Moab and the Israelites in the desert.

Elijah the Slave

Once there was a very poor man who had a large family to
support. It happened that several days before Passover, when
most Jews were preparing for the Seder and the great holiday of
Pesach, this poor man had nothing in the house, not even a piece
of Matzah. He tried to earn some money so as to be able to
observe the Seder like any other Jew, but he had no luck. He
stood in a corner of the market place and cried. Suddenly he felt
a hand touch his shoulder. When he turned around, he saw a
stranger standing near him. "Why are you crying?" asked the
stranger. "Because my children are hungry and I do not have
even one *prutah* to be able to observe Pesach," answered the Jew.

"Then sell me as a slave, and with the money which you will
receive for me, you will be able to celebrate Pesach," suggested
the stranger.

"But how could I celebrate the holiday of freedom by taking
away your freedom?" asked the Jew.

"Don't worry, just do what I am asking you."

The poor man sold the stranger to a prince, who paid 80 gold
dinars for him. The Jew observed the Seder in style, and then
used the rest of the money to start a business. He became a rich
man.

The slave who was sold to the prince was asked by his master,

"What is your specialty?" The stranger answered, "I am a builder and architect."

"Then build me a palace, and if you complete the work in three months, I will give you your freedom", said the master.

The next morning the prince was surprised to see a beautiful palace standing on his grounds, completely furnished. The prince then gave the slave his freedom.

As the slave disappeared, the prince saw letters of fire spell out the words: "Elijah the Tishbite." The prince then knew that his slave was really Elijah the Prophet, who would, in time to come, announce the coming of the Messiah.

The Magician

In one of the small towns of Poland there appeared one bright morning a magician, a very strange one. He was dressed in rags, but he had a stovepipe hat on his head. He never ate and never slept anywhere. When asked where he came from, his answer was, from Paris. Where was he going? To London. By way of Poland? He suddenly disappeared and reappeared on the other side of the street.

One day he hired a big hall in town and performed unbelievable tricks. From his mouth, he kept pulling out all kinds of silks. From his shoes, he pulled live turkeys. He bent down and began to scoop up gold coins; he whistled, and rolls and breads began to fly in mid-air. He whistled again and everything disappeared. Even though it was before Passover, when Jews are busy preparing for the holiday, still they found time to come and see the tricks of the strange magician. Just like the magicians of Egypt, they thought.

However, we shall leave the magician for a few moments and turn to Chaim Jonah who was once a rich lumber merchant. However, times had changed and he became poor. There were many times when his wife Beila had to sell some of her belongings to buy food for themselves. Even though they had no children, they suffered greatly. Chaim and Beila, remembering old times, tried to hide their poverty. They gave some of their hard-earned money to charity instead of buying food, so that their friends would not know the truth.

Sometimes Beila's neighbors tried to help her, but she refused, claiming that she had everything she needed. On Friday afternoons, she made a fire in her stove, even though she had nothing to cook, so that the smoke from the chimney should fool her neighbors.

When Passover came, Chaim and Beila drank the bottom of the cup of grief. They had no Matzoth, no wine, not even candles. Both sat in one room crying in the darkness.

Suddenly they heard a knock on the door. Chaim opened the door, and for a while could not see anyone in the dark. But he heard a man's voice asking permission to spend the Seder night with them, as he was a stranger and had no place to stay.

Chaim invited him in but explained to him that although he would be delighted to have him as a guest, unfortunately they themselves had nothing in the house.

Do not worry about the Seder," the stranger said, "I brought the Seder with me."

With a flip of his fingers, candles appeared in candlesticks of gold. He then motioned to the table in the corner. Chaim suddenly recognized the magician.

"Cover yourself, my dear table, in honor of Passover," the magician said. The table moved to the middle of the room, and from nowhere a white linen tablecloth appeared and covered the table. The stranger moved his hand, and the best foods appeared on the table. All Chaim and Beila had to do was to sit down and observe the Seder of Passover.

However, there was one hitch: According to law, you are not allowed to enjoy anything produced through black magic. The

Bible warns against it. Both decided to run to the rabbi's house and ask his advice, leaving the magician alone in their home.

The rabbi pondered the question, and then he said, "Anything produced by black magic could not be touched and handled, since all of it is just a deception and an illusion. Return to your home and see. If the Matzoth can be broken, and the wine poured in the glasses, and everything can be touched, it is not black magic, but Elijah the Prophet has come as a magician to help you."

When they returned home, they were overjoyed to find that everything could be touched. They realized that Elijah the Prophet had done all this for them. They were thus able to observe Pesach like all the other Jews.

(I. L. PERETZ)

PASSOVER QUESTIONS

Draw a Line Under the Correct Answer

Miriam was an Egyptian princess, the sister of Moses, a queen.

Amram was the father of Moses, his grandfather, his brother.

Aaron was the brother of Moses, his uncle, his son.

The Fier Kashes are four questions, four brothers, four sisters.

Seder is the name of a book, order of a celebration, name of a Jewish leader.

Maoth Chitim is charity, name of a place, name of a writer.

Bedikath Chometz is searching for Chometz, eating Chometz, burning Chometz.

Maror is the same as Charoseth, bitter herbs, sweet herbs.

Hillel was a great rabbi, first sandwich maker, wood cutter.

True or False

Passover is the holiday of fruit.

Passover is celebrated in Nissan.

Pesach is celebrated for two days.

We eat Matzoth on Pesach.

Moses took the Jews out of Egypt.

We celebrate Passover because the Jews entered the land of Canaan.

Elijah was a general.

Kashe means a question.

Why

Why do we drink four cups of wine?

Why do we put a fifth cup of wine on the Seder table?

Why do we sell our Chometz before Passover begins?

Why do we eat Matzoth on Pesach?

Why do we eat bitter herbs?
Why do we eat Charoseth?
Why do we dip twice?
Why do we put three Matzoth on the Seder table?
Why do we eat the Afikomen?
Why do we use hard-boiled eggs?
Why do we use salt water?

What is

Charoseth, Kneidlach, Seder, Fier Kashes, Maoth Chitim, Chad Gadyah, Karpas, Hagadah, Mechirath Chometz, Bedikath Chometz, Biur Chometz, Chometz, Shir Hashirim, Omer.

General Questions

Why do we celebrate Passover?
When do we celebrate Passover?
How many days do we celebrate Pesach?
Give three other names for Passover.
When do we start counting the Omer?
What is the Afikomen and why do we eat it at the end of the meal?
What is Chol Hamoed?
What portion of the Pesach celebration makes the biggest impression upon you?
Why do you like Passover?
Which part of the celebration do you like best?
Why is it so important to celebrate Passover every year?
Could you compare the Passover story to another historical happening?
How did you celebrate Passover last year?
Who asked the Kashes in your home last year?
Who conducted the Seder in your home?

What Do the Following Symbolize

Matzah, Maror, Charoseth, four cups of wine, karpas, salt water, 5th cup, Afikomen, Chad Gadyah, parsley, Passover.

Yom Ha'atzmaut

(INDEPENDENCE DAY)

The youngest of Jewish holidays is Yom Ha'atzmaut, Independence Day. It is celebrated on the fifth day of the Hebrew month of Iyar (May). This holiday marks the Athchalta D'Geula, beginning of the redemption, which was promised by God, and which religious Jews prayed for during the last eighteen hundred years. In our time, we were privileged to see how it came about.

The Story of Yom Ha'atzmaut

Ever since the Second Temple in Jerusalem was destroyed by the Romans in the year 70 C.E. (common era), and the Jews were driven out of Palestine, the Jews mourned. Every year on the ninth day of the Hebrew month of Ab, they fasted, sat in stockinged feet in the synagogue, and cried over the destruction of their Temple and country. In their prayers, they recited, three times a day, the prayer "Vesechezena Aynanu B'Shuvcha L'Zion B'rachamim" ("May we behold Your return in mercy to Zion").

For more than eighteen and a half centuries, Jewish leaders like the great rabbi Rambam and the great poet Yehuda Halevi spoke and wrote about the rebuilding of the Jewish temple. They also went up to the Land of Israel to live there. Many were the false Messiahs that appeared during this time and said they would lead the Jews back to Palestine. But it was not till the 19th century that an organized movement began for settling the Land of Israel.

In the 19th century, anti-Semitic movements developed in Europe. This led to the development of the Chibat Zion (love of Zion) movement which was sponsored by the leading rabbis, Rabbi Zvi Hirsch Kalischer and Rabbi Judah Alkalai. This movement urged the Jews to return to Palestine where they could worship God without attack by their neighbors. Small groups of Jews began to settle in Palestine. Sir Moses Montefiore of England and Adolph Crémieux of France helped the Jews settle in Israel.

The growing hatred of the Jews by the European anti-Semites caused Dr. Theodore Herzl, a Viennese journalist, to interest himself in the idea of returning to Palestine. In 1897, he called the first Zionist Congress in Basle, Switzerland, which organized the World Zionist Organization for this purpose. Dr. Herzl travelled to see the German Kaiser, the Turkish Sultan, and other leading statesmen to get their help, but without success. He succeeded in interesting large numbers of Jews in the Zionist Organization, and they carried on his work after his death.

At the end of the First World War on Nov. 2, 1917, the leaders of the World Zionist Organization got the British government to issue the famous Balfour Declaration. It said that the British government favored the establishment of a national homeland for Jews in Palestine, and would try to help the Jews reach this goal.

The British army captured Palestine, and the British government was given the duty of developing the country and aiding Jewish immigration. Soon, however, the British found that the Arabs were opposed to Jewish settlement in Palestine. As the Jews began to develop settlements in all parts of the country, and to introduce new farming, new industry, new economic, cultural and educational undertakings, the Arab opposition grew into murderous attacks on Jewish activities. The British, too, were taken aback by the rapid development of the country, and often sided with the Arabs. To defend themselves, the Jews developed an underground army known as the Haganah (Defense).

The country grew, but relations between the Jews and Arabs became even worse. The British gave in to the Arabs, and often appointed Commissions to study the problem. After every investigation, the report that followed usually took away from the Jews the right to bring more Jews into the country, and to buy land for settlement. The Jews refused to accept these reports and brought in illegal immigrants.

The Second World War stopped this inner fight, for everyone was busy fighting Hitler. But after the end of the war, the struggle against Britain and the Arabs grew. The British then brought the question to the United Nations. On November 29, 1947, the United Nations voted to partition Palestine, and to set up a Jewish state in one part of it.

The Jews were very happy about this U. N. decision. The Arabs were very angry and began attacking Jewish settlements; the surrounding Arab countries of Syria, Lebanon, Jordan and Saudi Arabia threatened war as soon as the English left Palestine, and the Jewish state was set up. The English helped the Arabs by leaving them arms. They also announced that on May 15, 1948, they would withdraw all English troops from Palestine.

On Friday, Hay Iyar (the fifth day of the Hebrew month of Iyar)—(May 14, 1948), the representatives of the Jewish settlement in Palestine met in Tel Aviv and signed a proclamation setting up the State of Israel; 1,878 years after the destruction of the Second Temple, the Jews regained their independence.

At midnight of May 15, 1948, when British rule ended, the armies of the neighboring Arab states invaded Israel. A fierce series of battles followed, and the Arab armies were defeated and sent reeling in disorder to their countries. The U.N. intervened and drew up an armistice which put an end to the fighting. The entire world rang with praise for brave little Israel.

The rabbis proclaimed Hay Iyar as the religious holiday of Yom Ha'atzmaut, Independence Day, to be observed with special synagogue services and prayers of thanks to God, not only by the Jews of Israel, but by Jews throughout the world.

SPECIAL CUSTOMS OF YOM HA'ATZMAUT

1. If the fifth day of Iyar comes on a Friday, then Yom Ha'atzmaut is celebrated on the day before, on Thursday.

2. It is customary to dress in holiday clothes on this holiday, and to go to the synagogue for a special evening service on the eve of the fifth day of Iyar, and a special service the next day. The order of these services has been set by the Chief Rabbinate in Israel. Special psalms of thanksgiving to God are sung. Holiday candles are lit in the synagogue before the evening service.

3. Toward the close of the evening service, one long blast is blown on the shofar (ram's horn) and the cantor and congregation say aloud: "May we be privileged to celebrate this holiday next year in Jerusalem rebuilt." Then a short prayer is said for the redemption and rebuilding of all of Jerusalem and Israel.

4. Jews greet each other with the traditional holiday greeting, Chag Sameach—Happy Holiday.

5. After the evening service, a holiday feast is served, accompanied by songs of praise and thanks to the Almighty.

6. In the morning service of Yom Ha'atzmaut, special holiday hymns are included as well as Hallel (Psalms of Praise), which is said on all holidays. A special memorial prayer is chanted for those who fell in the Israeli War of Independence, and another prayer for the welfare of Israel. A prominent guest or the rabbi delivers the sermon of the day.

7. The luncheon served after the morning service is a festive holiday meal.

8. It is customary to distribute charity to the needy on this day, as a sign of our thankfulness and appreciation to God, the provider of the poor.

9. In Israel, Yom Ha'atzmaut is celebrated in the large cities by impressive parades, in which contingents of all the branches of the Israeli armed services participate.

TALES OF INDEPENDENCE DAY

The Happy Decision
(FROM THE DIARY OF AN EYEWITNESS)

That Friday, all Jews in Palestine sat glued to their radios. One question was uppermost in their minds: Will the U.N. in New York vote to divide Palestine into separate Jewish and Arab countries? I felt the tension wherever I went in Tel Aviv. No decision had been reached when the Sabbath came.

Saturday night—still no decision, and the radio announced that the session would most probably be put over to the next day. I decided to go to bed.

At one o'clock in the morning, I was awakened by the tooting of horns and shrieks of sirens. I dressed hurriedly, and went out to the street. Shouts were heard on all sides. "The U.N. has decided in our favor!"

I saw people hurrying towards the Great Synagogue on Allenby Road, and I joined them. In the synagogue, a capacity congregation was saying Hallel (Psalms of Praise) with great fervor. At the conclusion of the Hallel, I went out again to the street.

In the large square before the Mugrabi Theatre, young people in great numbers were dancing horas to the accompaniment of Hebrew songs. Elsewhere, large trucks crowded with young, excited people were cruising through the streets.

By three o'clock, I decided to get some sleep, knowing well that the celebration would continue all of the next day.

The next day, I rose early to go to Ramat Hasharon. On the streets, all cars were decorated with Jewish flags and bunting. There was no school, and young and old were in a festive mood, singing and dancing. British tanks which only a few days before had menaced passing Jews, now flew Jewish flags on their gun turrets. Children of all ages got free tank rides, and British soldiers were relaxed, joining in the fun.

The bus to Ramat Hasharon travelled leisurely through the crowded streets. On the outskirts of Tel Aviv, the bus stopped before a table creaking under bottles of Palestinian wine. Several men boarded the bus with bottles of wine and glasses, and each passenger was asked to drink and toast the important event. Strangers clinked glasses with a hearty "L'Chayim," and wished each other a Happy Holiday.

I had just entered the office of Ramat Hasharon, when a call came through reporting the first Arab attack on a convoy from Tel Aviv to Jerusalem. The first Jews had been killed, and the general alert was sounded.

The celebration in the colony continued. The school children were lined up in front of the school for the ceremony of planting two trees on this great holiday. As a guest, I was given the privilege of planting one tree. I felt deeply moved as my shovel filled in the earth around the roots of the sapling.

Later in the afternoon, returning to Tel Aviv, we passed an

Arab village on the move. The men, women and children were carrying their tents and other belongings. They were cursing and spitting in our direction. As our bus passed, some Arab boys threw rocks at it, but no one was hit. The rage and anger on the faces of those Arabs foretold the bloody fight that was ahead. But at the moment, every Jew was still overjoyed by the Great Decision.

I. M.

The Evacuation

The British army was being evacuated and tension increased. Contact with the outside world ceased. The Arabs were becoming belligerent.

On March 21, a small convoy left the village of Kvutzat Nitzanim. A few moments later, a terrific explosion was heard. The convoy had hit a mine. After this, contact with other farms ceased completely.

The Arabs began to shoot daily. The children learned to stretch out on the ground, as soon as shooting was heard, no matter where they were.

This life of terror lasted for weeks. Over the radio, the entire population of the village heard of the Proclamation of the State of Israel by Ben Gurion. Song and dance followed this news, which was suddenly interrupted by Arab snipers.

The next day, an order was received to evacuate all children from the village, as the Arab armies were rolling in from all sides, and they were known to kill every one, man, woman and child.

The children were prepared for a night hike. The mothers said good-bye to their children, and so did the fathers who remained to defend the village. Only the most experienced and daring young men and women led the children, the men and women carrying the babies, and the older children holding on to the small children. All walked in silence, listening to every sound, every rustle, because they knew that there were snipers all around. The men and women holding the babies watched every baby carefully, lest it cry or make any noise. From afar, shots were heard and rockets shattered the silence. There was complete darkness all around. One false step on the winding, rocky road, and the whole chain of children might be hurled into the deep below. The children acted like real troopers, for they realized their dangerous situation.

Finally, they reached B'er Tuvia. Warm homes were waiting for them. The children were saved.

The Fall of Gush Etzion

Gush Etzion was a cluster of religious colonies which protected the road to Jerusalem and to Tel Aviv against the Arab invaders of Israel. Even if Gush Etzion had not existed, that defense point would have had to be established by the Haganah. True, Gush Etzion finally fell to the onrush of the overwhelming Arab Legion, but not before it fulfilled its task of giving the other units of the Haganah time to organize the defense of Jerusalem and other important sections. By delaying action, Gush Etzion saved the Jerusalem area for the State of Israel.

On March 27th, 1948, Gush Etzion was established as the central point of defense for the whole Jerusalem district. Greatly outnumbered, with restricted supplies of ammunition, about 170 Haganah defenders formed the core of the defense. A plan of strategy was worked out, not only of defense, but of attack, to disrupt the enemy communications and thus delay their attack on Jerusalem and Tel Aviv.

The plan was very successful in the beginning, until the British began to help the Arabs in their activities. On May 4, 1948, eleven days before the end of the British mandate over Palestine, heavy artillery directed by British officers in the Arab Legion began to shell the Haganah positions, and this bombardment was followed by many British Sherman tanks trying to break through to Gush Etzion.

The Haganah defenders realized the importance of their position, and decided to hold out to the last man. Many defenders were killed or wounded, but the post remained in the hands of the Haganah.

On May 12, two days before the expiration of the British Mandate over Palestine, the Arabs, led by a British colonel, launched a decisive attack. There were over 10,000 Arabs against 100 defenders. An armored column of the Arab Legion, after a heavy battle, reached Kfar Etzion. The enemy tried four times to break through to the center of Gush Etzion, but was repulsed with heavy losses.

The next day, twenty people with two Bren guns held out against sixteen attacks. Finally, the stand against the Arabs, led by the British, became desperate. The defenders decided to get the children out to a safer place, and then fight from house to house, knocking out tanks with Molotov cocktails (bottles filled with kerosene).

During the night, the children were bundled up and taken over difficult terrain to a safer place. The battle for Gush Etzion grew fiercer. To hold out further was impossible. The defenders contacted Jerusalem, and with its consent, signed a truce with the Arabs. They were taken prisoner by the Arab Legion, but not before they had attained their goal of giving the Jerusalem Jews a chance to conquer and hold the section of New Jerusalem for the newly established State of Israel.

Lag BaOmer

Lag BaOmer is a half-holiday celebrated by the Jews on the 18th day in the Hebrew month of Iyar (May). The meaning of the word LaG is 33 (Hebrew letter Lamed equals 30, and Hebrew letter Gimmel equals 3). LaG BaOmer means 33 days in the counting of the Omer.

Counting of the Omer

An Omer was an ancient measure of barley equal to a basket that held about 43 eggs. On Passover, the barley, which was planted in the winter, began to ripen.

Each farmer brought an Omer of this first ripe barley to the Temple on the second day of Passover. On the day that he brought the Omer, he would begin counting the Omer as the

Torah commanded him to do. He would say, today is the first day in the (counting of the) Omer. He would count 49 days, and the fiftieth day would be the Shavuoth holiday.

Lag BaOmer reminds us of the struggle of the Jews against the Roman rule during the 2nd century C.E. (common era).

Lag BaOmer is called the "Scholars' Holiday," because on this 33rd day of the counting of the Omer, the plague among the students of Rabbi Akiba stopped.

Lag BaOmer is also known as the Feast of Rabbi Shimon Bar Yochai. On this day, the Roman enemy was defeated and withdrew. Bar Yochai then left the cave in which he and his son Rabbi Eleazar had been hiding.

THE STORY OF LAG BaOMER

Rabbi Akiba

Rabbi Akiba, who was the leader of the revolt against the Romans, was an ignorant shepherd in his youth. He worked for a rich man called Kalba Savua. Savua's daughter, Rachel, fell in love with Akiba, the poor shepherd. She agreed to marry him on condition that he promise to study and become a learned man. Akiba, at the age of 40, went away to study in a Yeshiva for many years, and his wife Rachel lived in great poverty because her father disowned her.

Akiba became the most famous rabbi of his time, and he returned home with 24,000 pupils. The people of the city gave Rabbi Akiba a warm welcome. During the festivities, a poor woman tried to approach Rabbi Akiba, and his pupils wanted to stop her. Rabbi Akiba, however, called out, "Let her come near, she is my wife! Everything I know belongs to her because she urged me to study."

The Revolt of Bar Kochba

During the reign of the Roman Emperor Hadrian (117-138 C.E.), Rabbi Akiba, one of the greatest sages of that time, began a revolt against Rome. He chose a highly skilled commander, Bar Kochba, to lead the army, and Rabbi Akiba's pupils were the officers.

In the beginning, the revolution succeeded so well that the Romans left all of Judea, Samaria and Galilee in the hands of the rebels. But after several years of independence, the Bar Kochba revolution was crushed by Hadrian's general, Julius Severus.

The defeat of Bar Kochba was brought about by two causes. First, there were spies and traitors in Palestine who betrayed the country to the Romans. Secondly, a plague started, and every day a large number of Rabbi Akiba's pupils died. Only on the 33rd day of the counting of the Omer, the plague stopped.

Because of the plague, the army lost many leaders. Finally, the country was reconquered by the Romans.

Rabbi Shimon Bar Yochai

During this period, the Romans wanted the Jews to worship Roman gods, and not to teach the Jewish religion. The great sage Rabbi Shimon Bar Yochai, also known as Bar Yochai, defied the Romans and organized schools for Jewish children. There he and his son, Rabbi Eleazar, taught the Torah. The Romans found out about this and tried to catch and kill them. Bar Yochai and his son ran away and hid in a cave for 12 years.

Miraculously, a carob tree grew in front of the cave, and a spring of water appeared. So they ate carobs and drank the water while they studied the Torah.

Their little pupils would come to visit them, to bring them food, and study with them. In order to fool the Romans, the Jewish children took with them bows and arrows and baskets of food, so that it would seem they were going on a picnic. This is why it is a custom for Jewish children to go on picnics on Lag BaOmer.

One day, Bar Yochai saw a bird escape from a net. He took it as a sign from God that the Emperor was dead and they could return home. When they returned, they found that the symbol of the bird and the net had truly foretold their fate.

SPECIAL CUSTOMS FOR LAG BaOMER

1. The days of the counting of the Omer are considered sad days, and no parties or weddings are permitted during this period. However, on Lag BaOmer there are usually many weddings and other celebrations that could not take place on the other days.

2. Picnics and outings are arranged for Hebrew schools and Jewish children on Lag BaOmer. This is done in memory of the trips that Jewish children made to Bar Yochai's cave to study Torah.

3. In Israel, tens of thousands of Jews make a pilgrimage to Miron, a village in the hills of Safed. There, at the grave of the great Rabbi Shimon Bar Yochai, they pray, sing and dance. They make a great bonfire in memory of Bar Yochai and keep it burning all night while they sing and dance.

LAG BaOMER FOLKLORE

The Emperor Hadrian

Once, when Emperor Hadrian (who fought against Bar Kochba) passed along the street, a Jew greeted him. So Hadrian ordered the Jew to be killed because the Jew dared to talk to him.

On another occasion, another Jew who met Hadrian, knowing that one Jew was killed because he had greeted Hadrian, stood silent. Hadrian ordered that Jew be killed because he did not greet him.

When Hadrian was asked why he killed this Jew, he answered, "I am interested in killing all Jews, and no matter what they do I'll find an excuse to kill them."

The Death of Rabbi Akiba

After the Roman Emperor Hadrian crushed the Bar Kochba revolt, he began to hunt even more for Rabbi Akiba, who was the moving spirit of the revolt. In the meantime, Hadrian strengthened his decree that no Jew should study the Torah or teach it on pain of death.

A man by the name of Pappus came upon Rabbi Akiba as he was studying the Torah. Said Pappus to Rabbi Akiba, "Are you not afraid of the Romans that you defy their decree?"

Rabbi Akiba answered, "Let me tell you a parable. A fox once walked along the banks of a river, and he saw fish swimming back and forth as if disturbed or in fear of something. So he said to the fish, 'Why are you trembling so with fear? If you are afraid of nets or of other menaces in the water, come up on the dry ground out of the water, and you will not have to fear anything in the water.'

"The fish answered, 'You are supposed to be the cleverest living animal in the world, but you talk foolishly. If we are afraid for our lives in the water where we are at home, surely we should be more afraid on dry land where we will die for lack of water.' And so," continued Rabbi Akiba, "If we are in danger when we do study the Torah which is our staff of life, how much greater is the danger should we stop studying the Torah?"

Rabbi Akiba was finally seized by the Romans. He was condemned to death for participating in the revolt of Bar Kochba. Because he defied the Roman ban on Torah study, the Romans decided to punish him with a slow death. They combed his flesh with very sharp iron combs. However Rabbi Akiba did not utter a sound, but stood with a happy smile on his lips. His horrified pupils, who were standing by, wondered at Rabbi Akiba's calm behavior. They called out to their famous teacher, "Rabbi Akiba, how can you smile at such a terrible moment?" Rabbi Akiba answered, "All my life I wanted to be able to comply with the commandment that if necessary a Jew should give his life for God. Now that I am able to do so, I feel very happy." Rabbi Akiba died while saying the words, "Listen O Israel, the Lord our God the Lord is One."

Bar Kochba

When the Roman Emperor Hadrian oppressed the Jews harshly, they rose in revolt against the Roman Empire. The real hero of the revolt was Bar Kozba. Rabbi Akiba, who was the moving spirit of the revolt, was so impressed with Bar Kozba that he gave him the name of Bar Kochba, meaning a star (Kochav in Hebrew).

Bar Kochba was such a powerful man that he used to throw back with his knees the large stones which the Romans hurled at the Jews by means of throwing machines (catapults).

Thousands of Jews from different countries came to Bar Kochba to enlist in his army. But Bar Kochba did not accept everyone. He would test every recruit first. If an applicant would without complaint have his thumb cut off, he would be eligible for the army of Bar Kochba. The result was that the sages complained that Bar Kochba was maiming thousands of Jews. Instead, they suggested that the test should consist of uprooting a cedar tree while riding on a horse.

Bar Kochba followed the advice of the sages, and he eventually had 200,000 soldiers who could uproot a tree while riding on a horse.

Bar Kochba defeated the Roman army sent against him, and Hadrian felt that Bar Kochba, of the small country of Judea, was becoming a real menace to Rome. He summoned Severus, his best general, to fight against Bar Kochba. Severus realized that in open battle Bar Kochba would defeat him as he had defeated other Roman generals, but in delaying battles, he might win. His tactics were successful. Finally, Bar Kochba retreated to Betar, a stronghold in the mountains where the Romans could never get him, and where Bar Kochba could stay for years. Hadrian was about to give up and return to Rome. However, something happened which changed his plans.

In Betar, there lived a pious man by the name of Eliezer. He would pray to God every day that Betar should not fall into the hands of the Romans, and it was said that, because of him, Betar held out.

A traitor, a Samaritan who wanted the Romans to win, approached Eliezer and pretended to whisper in his ear. Some people who saw them became suspicious of this behavior, and reported it to Bar Kochba, who demanded of Eliezer that he tell what the Samaritan had whispered to him. Eliezer, who had hardly noticed the Samaritan because he was absorbed in prayer, replied that he did not know what this was all about.

Enraged, Bar Kochba ordered Eliezer killed, because he suspected him of treachery. As soon as Eliezer died, the Romans found a way to enter Betar. Soon a soldier found the body of Bar Kochba. When it was examined, they found a snake curled around it. It was a snake that killed Bar Kochba, not the Romans.

Most of the Jews of Betar were killed, and the revolt was

crushed. However, a number of Jews hid in mountain caves from which the Romans could not dislodge them. Only last year, these caves were discovered, and many utensils and scrolls of those Bar Kochba soldiers were found.

LAG BaOMER QUESTIONS

True or False

Rabbi Akiba was a great rabbi.
Bar Kochba was a Roman general.
Bar Yochai fought against the Romans.
The Romans called Judea Palestine.

Why

Why did the Jews revolt against the Romans?
Why did Rabbi Akiba choose Bar Kochba to lead the Jews?
Why did Rabbi Shimon Bar Yochai hide in a cave?
Why did the Romans change the name of Judea to Palestine?
Why did Bar Kochba fail?
Why is the holiday called Lag BaOmer?
Why are no weddings allowed during the counting of the Omer,
    except on Lag BaOmer?
Why do we go on picnics on Lag BaOmer?

General Questions

What do you learn from the story of Lag BaOmer?
What would you have done if you would have been in Bar
    Kochba's place?
Do you go on a picnic on Lag BaOmer?
Why was it important for Jewish children to study the Torah then,
    and why is it important now?
Why is it important to celebrate Lag BaOmer?

Shavuoth

The holiday of Shavuoth comes on the sixth and seventh day of the Hebrew month of Sivan (May or June). The holiday has four names:

CHAG HASHAVUOTH Holiday of weeks, because it is celebrated the day after completing the count of seven weeks since the Omer was brought on the second day of Passover.

Z'MAN MATAN TORASEINU Season of the giving of the Torah. Moses received the Tablets of the Torah from God on Mount Sinai at this season.

CHAG HABIKKURIM Holiday of the first ripe wheat. In ancient Israel, the Jews brought their first ripe wheat to the Temple in Jerusalem as a sign of appreciation for what God did for them.

ECHAD M'SHALOSH REGALIM One of the three Walking Holidays.

Shavuoth was the second Walking Holiday, when all male Jews in the Land of Israel went up to the Temple in Jerusalem to celebrate the holiday, and to bring a gift.

The Story of Shavuoth

In the third month after the Jews had left Egypt, they arrived in the Sinai desert, and camped opposite Mount Sinai.

Moses then was told by God to gather the Israelites together and tell them, "You saw what God did to the Egyptians. Now he is ready to give you one of the most precious gifts ever given to mankind, the Torah. If you will obey his commandments, He will always be present to help you and guide you."

The Israelites answered, "Everything that God commands us to do, we shall do. 'Na'aseh V'Nishmah'—we agree to do even before we have listened."

Moses then gave the Jews two days to cleanse themselves, wash their clothes and prepare to receive the Torah on the third day. At the same time, Moses told them not to come too near Mount Sinai. From early morning, dense clouds covered the peak of the mountain, thunder and lightning were frequently seen and heard. The sound of the Shofar came very strong, and the top of the mountain was enveloped in fire and smoke. The Israelites at the foot of Mount Sinai stood in great awe.

Moses then went up alone on the mountain, and as he neared the top, a mighty voice announced the TEN COMMANDMENTS:

1. I am the Lord, your God, who brought you out of the land of Egypt.
2. You shall have no other god but Me.
3. You shall not take the name of God in vain.
4. Remember the Sabbath day to keep it holy.
5. Honor your father and mother.
6. You shall not kill.
7. You shall not commit adultery.

8. You shall not steal.

9. You shall not bear false witness against your neighbor.

10. You shall not want (covet) anything that belongs to another.

The Israelites standing at the foot of the mountain listened to these commandments, which contained ideals of justice, kindness, wisdom and peace, and agreed to observe them.

The Israelites returned to their tents and waited for Moses to come down from Mount Sinai. When he appeared, Moses was carrying the Ten Commandments incribed on two stone tablets.

The Story of Ruth

During the days of the Judges, there came a famine in the land of Israel. Elimelech, a rich man of the tribe of Judah, decided to move with his family to the neighboring country of Moab, until the famine in his own land was over.

His two sons met the two daughters of Eglon, the king of Moab, and fell in love with them. The two brothers married the two princesses, Ruth and Arpah. Elimelech died soon after his arrival in Moab, and his two sons died soon thereafter.

Naomi, their mother, remaining alone in a strange land, decided to return to Israel, to be among her own people. Ruth, one of the daughters-in-law, had accepted the Jewish religion in good faith when she had married Naomi's son. When Naomi decided to return to Israel, Ruth insisted on going with her in order to be among Jewish people, where she could practice Judaism. Naomi tried to dissuade her from following her, as Ruth had wealth in Moab, and in Israel she would perhaps have to suffer hunger. Ruth could not be made to change her mind, and she followed her mother-in-law, Naomi, to Israel. Arpah, Ruth's sister, did not want to leave her father's palace and remained in Moab.

Naomi and Ruth settled in Bethlehem, and Ruth gleaned ears

of grain in the fields outside of the city, in order to support Naomi and herself.

One day, Boaz, the owner of a field in which Ruth was gathering grain, happened to notice her, and fell in love with her. He learned that she was a relative of his and that she was devoted to the Jewish religion, and to her mother-in-law Naomi. He then married her.

Boaz was one of the judges of Israel at that time, and Naomi was happy to see her daughter-in-law Ruth being rewarded for her devotion to the Torah. Boaz and Ruth had a son by the name of Obed, who was the grandfather of David, the future great king of Israel.

Because of Ruth's devotion to the Torah, it was decreed to honor her once a year on Shavuoth, the day of the giving of the Torah, by reading the Scroll of Ruth, which tells the story of Ruth.

SPECIAL CUSTOMS AND PRACTICES OF SHAVUOTH

1. AKDAMOTH   A poem in praise of God written in the Aramaic language, which is read on Shavuoth in the Synagogue.

2. MEGILATH RUTH (the Scroll of Ruth)   On Shavuoth the beautiful story of Ruth, ancestress of King David, is read because David was born on Shavuoth. A Moabite princess, Ruth married a Jew in the land of Moab; when her husband died, she turned her back on a life of luxury to return to Israel and the Jewish religion with her mother-in-law, Naomi. She has become the symbol of loyalty and piety, because she chose a life of poverty in preference to giving up her religion and principles.

3. Synagogues and temples are decorated with greens and flowers, to remind us that this is an agricultural holiday.

4. Today Bikkurim, the first ripe fruit, are brought in Israel's villages and towns to special ceremonies, to express the people's thanks to God for all his gifts to them.

Special Dishes Eaten on Shavuoth

1. BLINTZES are a cheese pastry usually eaten on Shavuoth, the holiday celebrating the giving of the Torah and the summer harvest in Israel. They symbolize the Torah as being good as milk. They also symbolize the land of Israel which was once a land flowing with milk and honey.

2. MILK AND HONEY symbolize the land of Israel which the Bible tells us was a "land flowing with milk and honey."

3. SHALTENOSES are cold blintzes and are eaten on Shavuoth. This dish originated among the Lithuanian Jews.

TRANSLATION OF BLESSINGS FOR SHAVUOTH

FOR LIGHTING CANDLES

Blessed are You, Lord our God, King of the Universe, who sanctified us with His commandments and commanded us to light the festival candle.

Blessed are You, Lord our God, King of the Universe, who kept us alive and preserved us and enabled us to reach this season.

FOR WINE

Blessed are You, Lord our God, King of the Universe, creator of the fruit of the vine.

FOR THE TALITH

Blessed are You, Lord our God, King of the Universe, who has sanctified us with His commandments and commanded us to wrap ourselves in the fringed garment.

FOR BREAD

Blessed are You, Lord our God, King of the Universe, who brings forth bread from the earth.

SHAVUOTH FOLKLORE

The Modest Mountain

When it became known that God would deliver the Torah to Moses on one of the mountains, all the mountains began to fight for the honor.

The tallest mountain said, "The Torah should be given on me for I am the highest." The most impressive said, "On me the Torah should be given, for I am the most majestic." The craggiest mountain said, "Only I am worthy to have the Torah given on me, for I am lofty and inaccessible." Of all the mountains, only the smallest, Mount Sinai, said nothing.

Then the Voice of God was heard: "You all quarrel in vain. I shall not pick the highest, the mightiest nor the most impressive mountain, but the humblest and smallest mountain among you." And God chose Mount Sinai.

The Guarantors

Before God gave the Torah, he said to Moses, "The children of Israel have agreed to accept the Torah. However, I would like to have someone guarantee that the children of Israel will observe the laws of the Torah."

Moses told God's wish to the Israelites, and they answered, "Our ancestors, Abraham, Isaac and Jacob, will be our guarantors."

God answered, "Your ancestors lived in the past. I need someone who will give a guarantee now."

"Our prophets are pious enough to be a guarantee," said the Israelites.

"Your prophets may be good men, but they will not be strong enough to make you observe the Torah," answered God.

"We will then give you our children as assurance that we will observe the Torah," said the Jews.

"Your children are the best guarantee," replied God, and then commanded Moses to go up to Mount Sinai to receive the Torah.

SHAVUOTH QUESTIONS

Draw a Line Under the Correct Answer

Ruth was the mother of Jacob, the ancestress of King David, daughter of Abraham.

Naomi was Ruth's mother-in-law, her sister, her mother.

Omer is the name of a city, of a measure of grain, of a man.

Boaz was a farmer, banker, teacher.

Mount Sinai is in Israel, Egypt, Persia.

Shavuoth is celebrated in the month of Cheshvan, Adar, Sivan.

True or False

The Ten Commandments were written on parchment.

The Torah was given to Aaron.

The Torah was given on Mount Sinai.

The Torah was given on Shavuoth.

We make a blessing over the Lulav on Shavuoth.

Shavuoth is celebrated for ten days.

Shavuoth is an agricultural holiday.

We eat blintzes on Shavuoth.

Why

Why do we call the holiday Shavuoth?

Why is Shavuoth called the holiday of first fruits?

Why is Shavuoth called also the season of the giving of the Torah?

Why do we count the Omer from Pesach to Shavuoth?

Why do we read the Akdamoth on Shavuoth?

Why do we read the Scroll of Ruth on Shavuoth?

Why did Ruth and Naomi return to Judea?

Why do we honor Ruth every Shavuoth?

Why is Shavuoth important to each one of us?

Rosh Chodesh

The word month in Hebrew is "Yerach" from the Hebrew word "Yareach," meaning moon. This shows that the Jewish calendar is based on the orbit of the moon. The calendar consists of 12 months. In a leap year, it consists of 13 months, to even out the difference between the Jewish calendar and the general calendar, for our calendar contains 354 days, and the general calendar has 365 days. Some months in the Hebrew calendar contain 29 days, and others have 30 days.

The Jewish calendar as used today was finally adopted and arranged by Hillel the second, in 360 C.E. The names of the months are as follows: Tishri, Cheshvan, Kislev, Teveth, Shevat, Adar Alef, Adar Beth, Nissan, Iyar, Sivan, Tamuz, Av and Elul.

The word month in Hebrew is also "Chodesh," from the Hebrew "Chadash," meaning new. Rosh Chodesh means the beginning of the new month. During the days of the Temple, Rosh Chodesh was considered a very important holiday. The coming of Rosh Chodesh was announced by the blowing of trumpets. There were gatherings in the Temple, where special Rosh Chodesh sacrifices were brought. Families observed special Rosh Chodesh meals, and no work was performed on Rosh Chodesh. Even Rosh Chodesh candles were lit.

However, after the destruction of the Temple, Rosh Chodesh became a half holiday, where work was permitted. In the synagogue, however, at the morning services, Hallel is chanted, a portion of the Torah is read, and Musaf (additional) service is added. All this indicates that it is a holiday service.

At present, in the modern State of Israel, efforts are being made to revive the ancient glory of Rosh Chodesh. Schools hold Rosh Chodesh assemblies, at which reports of unusual achievements are given. Also awards for monthly achievements are presented. The award of the monthly flag for patriotic duty or for exceptional work for the Jewish National Fund is also made. Special Rosh Chodesh songs are sung, and the National flag is saluted.

It is customary to announce the coming of the new month on the Sabbath preceding Rosh Chodesh at the Sabbath morning service. The introduction to the announcement is as follows:

"May it be Your will, O God, our Lord and the Lord of our fathers, to usher in the coming month, so as to be full of goodness and blessing. God grant us a long life of peace, goodness, blessing, sustenance, health, respect, fear of sin, a life free of shame, a life full of prosperity and honor, of love for the Torah, a life in which the desires of our hearts shall be fulfilled for the good of all. Amen."

ROSH CHODESH QUESTIONS

Draw a Line Under the Correct Answer

Rosh Chodesh is the beginning of the month, of the year, of the week.

Hallel is a collection of psalms, of trees, of books.

The Hebrew calendar has 12, 13, 14 months.

The Hebrew calendar is based on the orbit of the moon, sun, earth.

Chadash means: new, old, black.

True or False

Chodesh and Yerach are the same.

Yoreach means the sun.

Chodesh is the name of a holiday.

The Jewish month consists of 28 days.

General Questions

What does "Rosh Chodesh" mean?

When do we observe the holiday?

How was it celebrated in ancient days?

How do we observe Rosh Chodesh in America?

How is Rosh Chodesh observed in Israel?

